"To the obsessive-compulsive disorder (OCD) : ... you. It separates you from the people you love, wc ... on the street. It tells you that your thoughts and feelings are wrong and gross, and everyone else must just be in on a joke you can't hear. In *Thriving in Relationships When You Have OCD*, Amy Mariaskin expertly demonstrates how to navigate and reconnect to the relationships impacted by the disorder. She brilliantly balances the compassion for those suffering with a charm and humor that never condescends. The book is an easy read that also takes the time to explore the often-confusing nuances of OCD, such as the relationship between avoidance and compulsive behavior. In this book, Mariaskin has identified a missing piece of the self-help literature and readers will find their OCD much less puzzling as a result."

> —**Jon Hershfield, MFT**, director of The Center for OCD and Anxiety
> at Sheppard Pratt

"If OCD is taking over your relationships, this book offers hope and guidance. Amy Mariaskin provides tools and suggestions for how to thrive in relationships based on the best available treatment for OCD—exposure and response prevention (ERP). This fantastic book fills a significant gap in the field, and I will be recommending it to my own clients!"

> —**Jonathan S. Abramowitz, PhD**, professor, and director of clinical
> training at the University of North Carolina at Chapel Hill

"OCD can impact relationships, and the quality of those relationships. That's why this book is so important. Amy Mariaskin has been a guest on my podcast for many years because of her insight and caring nature. Her new book aims to help you navigate many things, including the trap of reassurance and the pain that follows avoidance, while moving toward meaningful relationships of all kinds."

> —**Stuart Ralph**, psychotherapist for children and young people,
> and host of *The OCD Stories* podcast

"I discovered within these pages a more robust vocabulary to communicate with the people I love, and a deeper appreciation for the incredible OCD community to which I belong. My story was reflected back to me with warmth, empathy, and humor. I am incredibly grateful for this book!"

> —**Jason Adam Katzenstein**, *New Yorker* cartoonist, and author
> of *Everything Is an Emergency*

"A life well lived has rich, meaningful, and caring relationships with others! And yet, when a person struggles with obsessions, this basic need and natural capacity for connection are affected by confusion, doubt, and shame. But there is hope; there are skills you can learn to discover deeper intimacy with the ones that matter in your life.

Relationships, all of them, are the ultimate unknown. In this book, Amy Mariaskin will show you how to navigate relationship anxiety and obsessive doubts without losing yourself—in a compassionate and actionable way. There will be ups and downs in this learning process, and Mariaskin will prepare you to navigate all of those moments so you can thrive in your relationships. This is a must-read book for anyone dealing with OCD that wants to experience rich and fulfilling connections!"

—**Patricia E. Zurita Ona, PsyD**, author of *Acceptance and Commitment Skills for Perfectionism and High-Achieving Behaviors* and *Living Beyond OCD*

"The impact of OCD extends well beyond the individual with the disorder. Obsessions may be private events, but the attempt to cope with obsessions involves behavior that can significantly affect the lives of family, friends, and others. Amy Mariaskin's book eloquently explains the interpersonal damage that can be associated with OCD, and offers sound advice for promoting healthy relationships despite the challenges of OCD. Her book is a valuable contribution to the literature that will be immensely helpful to people with OCD and to the people who care about them as well."

—**C. Alec Pollard, PhD**, professor emeritus of family and community medicine at Saint Louis University School of Medicine, and founding director of the Center for OCD & Anxiety-Related Disorders at Saint Louis Behavioral Medicine Institute

Thriving in Relationships When You Have OCD

How to Keep Obsessions &
Compulsions from Sabotaging Love,
Friendship & Family Connections

AMY MARIASKIN, PHD

New Harbinger Publications, Inc.

Publisher's Note

This publication is designed to provide accurate and authoritative information in regard to the subject matter covered. It is sold with the understanding that the publisher is not engaged in rendering psychological, financial, legal, or other professional services. If expert assistance or counseling is needed, the services of a competent professional should be sought.

NEW HARBINGER PUBLICATIONS is a registered trademark of New Harbinger Publications, Inc.

New Harbinger Publications is an employee-owned company.

Copyright © 2022 by Amy Mariaskin
New Harbinger Publications, Inc.
5674 Shattuck Avenue
Oakland, CA 94609
www.newharbinger.com

All Rights Reserved

Cover design by Amy Shoup; Acquired by Elizabeth Hollis Hansen; Edited by Brady Kahn

---

Library of Congress Cataloging-in-Publication Data

Names: Mariaskin, Amy, author.
Title: Thriving in relationships when you have OCD : how to keep obsessions and compulsions from sabotaging love, friendship, and family connections / Amy Mariaskin, PhD.
Description: Oakland, CA : New Harbinger Publications, [2022] | Includes bibliographical references.
Identifiers: LCCN 2022028217 | ISBN 9781648480584 (trade paperback)
Subjects: LCSH: Interpersonal relations. | Obsessive-compulsive disorder. | Families.
Classification: LCC HM1106 .M373 2022 | DDC 616.85/227--dc23/eng/20220811
LC record available at https://lccn.loc.gov/2022028217

Printed in the United States of America

24   23   22

10   9   8   7   6   5   4   3   2   1   First Printing

To anyone with OCD who has felt alone.

May you find your people within these pages
and out in the world.

Contents

Foreword

One of the highlights of my career has been helping people with obsessive-compulsive disorder. People with OCD are courageous, incredibly smart, and mind-blowingly creative and witty. Simply put, they are my kind of people.

During their OCD treatment, clients often come to the session with a dilemma about one of their relationships. Maybe the difficulty is with a friend, family member, roommate, colleague, or intimate partner. They report feeling unsure of how to handle specific relationship situations because, in the past, their OCD has been 100 percent in the driver's seat, reminding them of the many "possible" scary outcomes that could occur. OCD has also been their rulemaker, forcing them to act only in response to fear, doubt, and uncertainty. But now that they are determined to overcome their OCD, they must find another way.

In these cases, I ask, "What would you do in this situation if anxiety or uncertainty was not present?" This is such a magical question!

Almost every time, they respond with a similar, yet original, answer: "I'd ask them on a date even despite my fears that they'll say no." "I'd go to the party on Saturday night. Of course, I would still have intrusive thoughts, but I wouldn't treat my thoughts as if they were important." "Instead of avoiding eye contact, I'd do my best to initiate a conversation with that work colleague." "I'd be more open with my partner. I would trust myself more."

I'm guessing you picked up this book because OCD has done precisely what OCD always does—impacted the things you value the most. OCD may have stolen your time and your confidence, holding you back from engaging in many different relationships throughout your life. OCD may have made you feel like an outsider, making it hard to connect with others. OCD may have convinced you that you are not worthy of relationships or love. If this has been the case for you, please know that you are not alone.

It is my honor to introduce *Thriving in Relationships When You Have OCD: How to Keep Obsessions and Compulsions from Sabotaging Love, Friendship, and Family Connections.* This book is a compassionate, evidence-based guide to managing the many types of relationships that you may be navigating. Whether it be friendships, dating, or any connection in your life, Amy provides a safe, knowledgeable, and inclusive approach to thriving in all your relationships. The fact that you opened this book and committed to investing in yourself is an act of courage, and I wildly celebrate you for that. As you move through each chapter, you will be one step closer to taking your life back from OCD and building successful, healthy relationships that support and nourish you.

As I read over this manuscript, I found myself excitedly nodding my head and whispering, "Yesss!" and "Thank you, Amy, for including that important point." Dr. Mariaskin consistently provides practical and actionable advice in a world where relationship advice can be extreme and counterproductive. While there are some wonderful resources out there for managing relationships, many authors forget that being in a relationship, especially while having OCD, requires a balanced and nuanced approach. We rarely ever thrive when we live in the black and white, and Amy teaches us how to live and thrive in our relationships while making room for the gray (uncertainty, fear, and doubt). Her advice is fundamental for OCD recovery and can help you go on to embrace a wide variety of enriching and values-based relationships.

It is more than likely that there will be moments when you want to close this book and crawl under the blankets. You may tell yourself that there is no hope for you or that you don't deserve love, because of your intrusive thoughts or compulsions. I want you to remember that this is not true. The intrusive thoughts you experience and compulsions you engage in do not disqualify you from being loved by others or offering your love to others.

As you embark on this journey, I would like to highlight a fundamental concept that Amy shares many times in this book. Never forget to be kind and compassionate as you ride the highs and lows of this work. There will be good days and hard days. Remember that small steps lead to medium-sized steps, and medium-sized steps lead to monumental-sized wins that will change your life. By giving yourself permission to take this journey one step at a time, you can find ways to cultivate and nurture a wide array of relationships (or just a few, if that is your preference) and design the life you deserve.

—Kimberley Quinlan, LMFT
Author of *The Self-Compassion Workbook for OCD*
and founder of CBTschool.com

Acknowledgments

In writing this book about relationships, I've been buoyed by many of my own supportive relationships. These are the people (and one dog) who kept me going in moments of self-doubt and encouraged me to dedicate myself to this project with curiosity and openness. I've been jokingly described as having a self-sufficiency kink, and these individuals showed me the value of relying on others. In some ways, this was the experiential counterpart to the writing: as I asked others to nurture their relationships, I likewise opened myself up to receiving care.

First, thank you to all my clients, current and past, who've trusted me to accompany them on their therapeutic journeys. Your wisdom is written into these pages, and your voices echo through mine. The relationships I've been privileged to forge with you have changed my notions of vulnerability, trust, reciprocity, and care.

Thank you to my New Harbinger team, Vicraj Gill, Elizabeth Hollis Hansen, Wendy Millstine, and Brady Kahn, who treated my writing with thoughtfulness and compassion, always challenging me to consider the best interests of the reader with each edit. You helped me convey the concepts of the book clearly while preserving my voice.

Thank you to my husband for reminding me about the joy of writing, making this book less like labor and more like play. You kept things in perspective and never doubted my ability to succeed. Thank you to Kimberley Quinlan for writing the foreword and being accessible for all my impostor syndrome–fueled questions and lamentations along the way. And thank you to my very first clinical supervisor, Ron Batson, who saw my potential to be a clinician even through the thick haze of anxiety and insecurity obscuring my own vision.

I'm endlessly grateful for my Nashville OCD & Anxiety Treatment Center colleagues, whose curiosity, creativity, and heart inspire me. Thank you to Kelly Flanagan, Mark Freeman, Jay Galante, Lynn and Ron Heady, Melissa Jean, Cassandra Marzke, Kat Ross, Sarah-Jean Russell, and Jenn Stewart for your feedback about drafts and for laughing at my corny jokes along the way. Finally, thanks to everyone else who made this possible by providing resources or just helping me to hold the messy feelings along the way: Becci, Jon, Nicole, Cleveland, Val, and Vanessa, to name a few. Finally, thank you for reading this book. I hope it shows you how lovable and capable of connection you are.

Introduction

Having obsessive-compulsive disorder (OCD) can be lonely. Worries may stop you from doing the things you love with the people you care about. Rituals may crowd out your free time. And shame may create a barrier to sharing your innermost thoughts. Going at it alone can feel like the safest way to move through the world. But in doing so, you're also stifling your ability to build and foster supportive relationships. I understand why it feels so hard to find your people when you have OCD, and I want this book to help dismantle some of the barriers on that journey, because you, my friend, have so much to offer. And relationships have so much to offer you.

Maybe you've seen the statistics on how long it takes most people to receive proper diagnosis or treatment for their OCD: a 2021 study found that, on average, almost thirteen years pass between when someone first experiences symptoms and when they're diagnosed (Ziegler et al. 2021). That's a startling number. A decade and then some! A golden retriever's average life span! And proper treatment takes even longer. I personally know all too well.

Seventeen—that's my number.

My first memories of OCD are from first grade. I remember crying into my chocolate milk as my babysitter asked me what was wrong. I was inconsolable after a classmate threw up at school, rendering the whole classroom dangerous in my mind. I shook my head and told her I had a headache, vowing internally that I would never drink that now-dirty-by-association brand of chocolate milk again. What compels a seven-year-old to hide the content of her worries, even as fat tears roll down her cheeks? No one told me it was embarrassing to have these worries, but I compared myself to other kids and reasoned that if they weren't concerned, I shouldn't be either. But I was. The world was full of things that scared or disgusted me: fire safety presentations at school, the thick odors of fried food mingling with the acrid tang of all-purpose cleaner in the school cafeteria, the grime that populated the seam between toilet and tiles in the bathroom, and the haunting sounds from river barges that wafted through my window at night. For years, OCD made me feel like I was living in a glass bubble, staring out at everyone else.

When as a graduate student I was given the diagnosis, I was floored. *OCD? What?* Even as someone studying to become a psychologist, I was uninformed about "real OCD." If you've had that experience too, you might be reluctant to take the risk of getting close to others. I'm proud of you for picking up this book anyway. First, let's talk a little bit about the structure of the book and where you can find the information you need.

Chapters 1 and 2 will introduce information about OCD and its treatment before examining ways that OCD and relationships can influence one another. Chapter 3 will review a few themes of OCD that focus on relationships specifically, providing activities to help manage these tricky symptoms. Chapters 4 and 5 will examine friendship and dating before chapter 6 delves into the impact of OCD on sex. Chapter 7 is about moving in with others, and chapters 8 and 9 are about family and parenting. Chapter 10 is about managing relationships at work. Although this is not a formal workbook with a structured plan, it includes activities and exercises for you to practice skills you'll pick up along the way. You will find the complete set of worksheets along with other helpful tools at http://www.newharbinger.com/50584.

Recovering from OCD is one of the toughest things anyone can do. It means opting to move boldly toward the life you want instead of running away from what you fear. It means taking a leap into the unknown. And having companionship when you take that leap can make all the difference. I hope this book will help you find the allies in your life who can cheer you on as you forge ahead toward the beautiful, complex, and full life that you deserve. Let's go!

CHAPTER 1

The Third Wheel
OCD's Role in Your Relationships

Obsessive-compulsive disorder has a major PR problem, and it's not what you might think. The problem is not that popular media gives OCD a bad rap but that it fails to explore the full range of hardships and the diversity of symptoms experienced by those with this disorder. Television characters with OCD appear rigid and persnickety, and their OCD is cast as a personality quirk—slightly irritating or lovably goofy—rather than a debilitating disorder. Characters with OCD often display mild cleaning or organizing behaviors, which is hardly an accurate picture of the full range of obsessive-compulsive symptoms. These misrepresentations have persisted despite about 2.3 percent of people meeting criteria for OCD over their lives (Ruscio et al. 2010). One out of every fifty people are seeing an extremely distorted mirror held up to themselves.

Before we dive in, there are a few important things to note. You didn't cause your OCD, and your OCD is certainly not your fault. Your symptoms are valid even if they seem irrational or bizarre. No one experiencing these painful and vexing symptoms would choose to have them, while it can also seem terrifying to let go of them. Ultimately, all the thoughts and behaviors that follow from having OCD are just part of your particular norm—a norm shared by millions of other people with similar brains. So, throughout the book, I'll use the term *OC-normal* to describe the thoughts, feelings, and behaviors that go along with having OCD.

Said another way, for people with OCD, the thoughts and behaviors we're discussing are the norm rather than the exception. Avoiding things with the letter H because you don't want to think about contracting HIV? OC-normal. Feeling like you have to maintain symmetry between your pinky toes? OC-normal. Thinking about throwing your baby down a staircase? OC-normal. Visualizing the whole thing over and over? Also OC-normal. And if your brain is now coming up with all kinds of *buts* and *what-ifs* in response to these examples, in an effort to prove that your OCD is the exception to the rule, guess what? That's OC-normal too. Using this phrase throughout the book will hopefully serve as a counterpart to pop culture's depictions of OCD. We will reclaim the true definition of the condition, page by page!

Understanding OCD

There are two primary components of OCD: obsessions and compulsions. *Obsessions* are unwanted and persistent thoughts, images, sensations, or urges that cause anxiety or distress. Obsessions can be focused in one area, such as experiencing unwanted thoughts solely about religious scrupulosity (worries about blaspheming, sinning, or otherwise violating your religious doctrine). But, more commonly, obsessions occur across several different themes, including but not limited to concerns about contamination, safety, aggression, symmetry, sexuality, identity, morality, and perfectionism.

Obsessions are intrusive and distressing, and people usually try various strategies to quell them. You might have experienced this yourself and discovered that these strategies often backfire, providing you with only temporary relief before the obsessions roar back with a slightly different nagging concern. One common and understandable strategy is to avoid anything that provokes the obsessions. Avoidance can be physical, as in refusing to go to playgrounds when intrusive thoughts about harming a child are present. However, avoidance can also be cognitive, emotional, or sensory, meaning that you begin to do mental gymnastics to avoid certain thoughts, feelings, and sensations that remind you of your worries.

It can be downright exhausting! You might carve out whole areas of your life to prevent obsessions, only to end up feeling drained and more defeated—especially when OCD affects your relationships or other important areas in your life.

One particularly insidious feature of obsessions is that, in most cases, you know that they're irrational or excessive in nature, and on top of experiencing distress at your "crazy" thoughts, you may feel that you need to hide those thoughts. The truth is that all human brains (even those without OCD) conjure up a multitude of bizarre, taboo, and intrusive thoughts every day. Therefore, even though your obsessions might feel like the primary issue to combat, they are not the most pressing one. And it's a good thing that we're not targeting your thoughts; research shows that attempts to suppress or eliminate thoughts are ineffective and may lead to even more intrusions (Wenzlaff and Wegner 2000). That's right—it's like running away from a rambunctious puppy—the thoughts are bound to chase you! Instead of going after the thoughts, it's the *response* to these thoughts that we're interested in changing, because the response perpetuates the obsessive-compulsive cycle.

Think of it this way. Imagine that you're sitting in a grassy field in the middle of summer. You feel a tickle on your leg and then a tiny pinch as a mosquito punctures the skin. Minutes later you feel the uncomfortable sensation of a welt appearing, followed by a wave of itchiness. You want relief, so you scratch it—at first gently and then vigorously as it gets itchier and itchier. Your body responds to the scratching and increased irritation, releasing histamines and creating more itchiness. With OCD, the mosquito bite represents your obsessions (annoying and difficult to ignore), and your compulsions are your attempts to scratch those pesky itches! You want to scratch to rid yourself of the distress, even though scratching won't ultimately help in the long run. Our goal then is to control the compulsion to scratch, because while you can't get rid of the bite or the urges to scratch, you can control the scratching itself.

Put another way, *compulsions* are repetitive behaviors or mental acts that reduce distress. Common compulsions include checking, cleaning, ordering or arranging, evening up, reassurance seeking, perfectionistic behaviors, counting, and researching. Just like scratching a mosquito bite, these behaviors may provide a bit of respite from your distress but won't make the obsessions go away. Compulsions can be invisible to others, as they can be mental as well as physical rituals. In fact, I've observed that ruminating, or mentally engaging with OC-relevant content, is among the most prominent symptoms for my clients with OCD. This can look like reviewing past interactions (the "postgame analysis"), attempting to analyze unanswerable questions, checking for internal sensations, imagining future scenarios, excessively praying, or other internal hoop-jumping.

Avoidance can even be a preemptive compulsion if you're using it to reduce the probability of coming into contact with your obsession. In that case, avoidance has the same effect as any other compulsion: scratching the proverbial itch and ensuring that the obsessive-compulsive cycle will continue. The paradox of compulsions is that the more you follow their rules to feel safe, avoid uncertainty, or attain a "just right" feeling, the farther you get from living the kind of life you want. In fact, the more you give in, the more OCD wants from you. By the time you learn all the steps that OCD demands, you're doing an awfully complicated dance with spins, jetés, and pirouettes. And maybe all you wanted to do was walk across the room to get a glass of water.

Breaking the OCD Cycle

In the end, treating OCD comes down to breaking this cycle of obsessions and compulsions. This is a matter of learning to tolerate the feelings and thoughts that drive compulsive urges so that those thoughts and feelings no longer steer your behavior and dominate your attention. In other words, you learn to stop acting on your compulsions.

But if performing compulsions feels like the only way to get relief, how does treatment actually work? For most people, the answer is slowly, at first. There's a lot that goes into unlearning patterns that may have persisted for years. So be gentle with yourself if you're new to treatment and it doesn't feel effortless. Any step toward transforming these patterns and reducing compulsions is a step toward recovery. Finding a therapist qualified to work with OCD can be a helpful part of the process too, and, thankfully, we have effective therapy options, many of which will be applied in this book.

EXPOSURE AND RESPONSE PREVENTION

Exposure and response prevention (ERP) is the research-backed treatment with the most evidence for treating OCD effectively (Olatunji et al. 2013). It works by helping people to engage with things that they've been avoiding or enduring with distress—through *exposure*—and reducing their compulsive responses in these situations—through *response prevention*. This may sound scary, and if you're skeptical, that's perfectly understandable. ERP can get a bad rap for being confrontational, but a skilled therapist would take things at a pace dictated by you. The saying at our clinic is "Don't start with the Rottweiler." If you had a dog phobia, we wouldn't start exposures with the most intimidating dog! Instead, you would interact with smaller and gentler dogs first and gradually build up your tolerance, Yorkie to Great Dane style.

ACCEPTANCE AND COMMITMENT THERAPY

Acceptance and commitment therapy (ACT) is another therapy with promising results for OCD treatment (Twohig et al. 2018). ACT is an action-oriented therapy that highlights the balance between accepting reality and enacting behavioral changes to live a life that aligns well with your values. In ACT, values are the concepts that connect you with the things that matter most to you. Adventure, humor, kindness, and curiosity are all examples of values. With this treatment, there's an emphasis on choosing new behaviors—not to rid ourselves of negative emotional experiences but to foster our engagement with the things we love doing. ACT therapists recognize, in fact, that much of our psychological suffering comes from pushing down unwanted emotions rather than accepting them as a necessary part of the human experience.

COGNITIVE BEHAVIORAL THERAPY

Both ERP and ACT fall under the umbrella of another three-letter acronym, CBT, or cognitive behavioral therapy. CBT posits that our thoughts, emotions, and behaviors all influence and are influenced by one another, and it concentrates on helping us flexibly try out alternative behaviors and thoughts or perspectives to reduce the impact of symptoms. If you're familiar with the term *black-and-white thinking*, you already know a little bit about how CBT helps to identify and change unhelpful thought patterns.

We will be using elements of CBT, ERP, and ACT throughout this book to help you reduce the impact of OCD on your relationships. We will also delve into other techniques, such as mindfulness and self-compassion, that can strengthen your ability to be present in your relationships and to reduce the impact of shame and self-stigmatizing on your connections with others.

Assessing Your OCD Themes

Are you ready to see what flavors of OC-normal make up your specific symptom picture? Here's a list of some common themes that occur in OCD along with examples of how these themes can impact your interpersonal relationships. Perhaps your OC-normal fits neatly into one or more of these common themes—or not. Take note that this list isn't exhaustive. There are as many flavors of OC-normal as there are people, and if your own example does not appear here, know that you just have a creative brain with its own OCD themes.

Contamination themes: worries about coming into contact with dirt, germs, bodily fluids, chemicals, or other contaminants; worries about sticky substances; concerns about contamination from people or places. *Possible relationship impacts*: rigid rules about your partner's cleaning practices; conflict about time spent in rituals; reluctance to join in social or work activities at certain locations; concerns about having children; avoidance of sexual intimacy; lateness to social events because of rituals; reluctance to let others into your space.

Harm themes: worries about inflicting harm on yourself or others accidentally or on purpose; worries about harm befalling others; unwanted and disturbing thoughts or images. *Possible relationship impacts:* avoidance of activities deemed risky (such as driving with a passenger in the car, cooking together with knives); difficulty being alone with certain people you've deemed "vulnerable"; difficulty sleeping near others because of fears of sleepwalking and harming; frequent checking to ensure safety.

Sexual themes: worries about being sexually attracted to family members, children, or pets; worries about acting out sexually. *Possible relationship impacts:* avoidance of sex; difficulty with physical closeness in platonic relationships; avoidance of certain groups of people; difficulty changing children's diapers or bathing them; secrecy and shame in relationships.

Identity themes: worries about having a different sexual orientation or gender than the one you have identified with thus far. *Possible relationship impacts:* withdrawing from people who trigger these thoughts; avoidance of intimacy; reluctance to engage in social activities that may "confirm" your feared identity; reassurance seeking.

Scrupulosity themes: worries about engaging in immoral behavior, having immoral or sinful thoughts, or breaking rules from your religious doctrine or moral code. *Possible relationship impacts:* excessive apologizing and reassurance seeking; scrutiny of loved ones' behaviors; worries about your loved ones' salvation; avoidance of places of worship; difficulty affiliating with people who challenge your morals; worries about offending partner; people pleasing.

Just right themes: having to have things a certain way (such as aesthetically, sensorily, mentally) to prevent either a negative outcome or an uncomfortable sensation. *Possible relationship impacts:* conflict about shared living spaces; rigid rules for others in the home; rituals taking time away from relationships; difficulty with timely work completion, leading to conflict.

Relationship themes: worries about your attraction to or love for your partner; concerns about compatibility in relationships; doubts about your partner's love for you (such doubts can also manifest in friendships and other relationships). *Possible relationship impacts:* reassurance seeking; conflict about privacy and boundaries; conflicts about trust issues; difficulties with commitment; conflict about perceived rejection; scrutiny of behavior in relationships; frequent bids for contact in times of separation.

Health themes: concerns about your physical or mental health; hypervigilance about bodily sensations or mental phenomena as an indicator of illness or injury. *Possible relationship impacts:* conflicts about finances related to doctor's visits; reassurance seeking; difficulty maintaining relationships with health care providers; avoidance of sexual intimacy; canceling plans due to worries about illness.

Hyperawareness or sensorimotor themes: focus on and hypervigilance of physical sensations such as blinking, swallowing, and breathing. *Possible relationship impacts:* difficulty remaining present in conversations and activities with loved ones; reassurance seeking; isolating because of worries about seeming awkward or preoccupied.

Existential themes: worries about large unknowable questions, such as the meaning of life, our place in the universe, and the nature of reality. *Possible relationship impacts:* reassurance seeking; frequent conversations to research these topics; avoidance of places of worship; difficulty accepting love or affection because of its impermanence; avoidance of certain media or activities.

Sometimes OCD themes can intersect, such as when someone believes that they must feel 100 percent alert (an example of the just-right theme) before cooking to avoid accidentally poisoning their family (which invokes both the harm and contamination themes). It may be that some of these themes resonate with you quite a bit while others are foreign to your experience. Take a moment to reflect on some of the ways that you experience OCD. Next we'll delve further into how OCD may be affecting you interpersonally.

Relationships and OCD

As much as some of us try to deny our need for connectedness, relationships are a fundamental part of being human. A baby is born with limited abilities beyond the autonomic processes that regulate temperature, breathing, heart rate, and basic sensory functions. For their needs to be met, others must provide food, shelter, safety, and an introductory course on relating to others. Indeed, humans have instinctive mechanisms that allow them to perceive and react to distress by providing both emotional and physical support.

Researchers who study attachment—the ways that we form bonds with others—have found that parents are able to attune their behaviors to the physical and emotional expressions of their babies within seconds (Feldman, Greenbaum, and Yirmiya 1999): proof that parents really are superheroes! For babies, and the children they eventually become, learning that others will be there to provide this support gives them the foundation from which to explore the world and take risks. This phenomenon, called *secure attachment,* allows them not only to receive emotional support as they're growing up but also to cultivate curiosity and pursue their interests. In this way, humans are fundamentally cooperative animals. And although the shape of our social needs changes over the life span, relationships and relatedness remain central to our functioning.

Presumably if you're reading this book, you're no longer a baby! Your relationships are probably far more varied than those in the infant world. You may be navigating dozens of important ones daily—with family members, your partner, your friends, and your coworkers—not to mention all the acquaintances and microrelationships that you encounter when making your way in the world. While we will concentrate only on the more significant relationships in your life (apologies to the grocery store cashier), we will explore how to recognize and reduce OCD's impact on the full expression of those different connections.

Confronting Relationship Barriers

OCD is rarely discussed as an interpersonal issue in the psychological literature. It's usually discussed as something that affects someone's individual functioning rather than the relationships in which that person is embedded. However, anyone with OCD will tell you that their disorder has a profound impact not only on their own thoughts, behaviors, and emotions but also on the lives of others who are close to them. It can root into these relationships, creating tension and conflict or stymieing intimacy. Families affected by OCD function differently from families without it. Loved ones often become enlisted in the rituals of people with OCD or find themselves walking on eggshells to prevent provocation. It's almost as if OCD is the third wheel in relationships: unwanted, disruptive, and more than a little annoying. OCD can create barriers both in the development of new relationships and in the maintenance of existing ones. The following are some examples of potential barriers that will be further explored in future chapters.

EMOTIONAL BARRIERS

Wherever there's OCD, anxiety is likely to tag along. This emotion, and its cousins terror, dread, and worry, can really put a damper on the natural development and maintenance of a relationship. Anxiety may

shine a light on the scariest of possibilities and make them feel like immi-
nent realities instead of improbable what-ifs. It can whisper all kinds of
stories in your ear about how your friends are mad at you, your partner is
cheating on you, or your therapist is going to fire you. Anxiety may undermine your confidence in advocating for a promotion at work or asking for
a flexible deadline with a project. Parents with OCD may find anxiety a
constant companion while helping their children explore a world that
feels rife with risk and danger.

Remember that despite a prevalence rate of about one in fifty, OCD
is often portrayed as a personality quirk, a simple tendency toward fussiness, and the butt of unfunny jokes. Therefore, it makes sense that some
people with OCD are reluctant to disclose their symptoms and may associate their symptoms with a sense of shame or embarrassment. As
someone with OCD, you may have experienced this when meeting new
people: *Will they reject me if they find out about my thoughts? Will I ever be
able to get close enough to someone to tell them about my OCD? How would
anyone be able to accept my rituals?* These feelings are entirely understandable. Often when people hear for the first time that their symptoms are
OC-normal, they experience an initial wave of relief, which is quickly
followed by the fear that only a therapist or a fellow sufferer will ever
understand what they're going through. This, too, may lead to withhold-
ing information about symptoms, which only reinforces the shame surrounding these symptoms.

Although guilt is a natural response to having done something that
conflicts with your personal values or morals, it can also arise unnaturally
in the context of OCD. You may have experienced feelings of guilt about
the OC-normal thoughts you experience, for example, even though you
didn't carry out any behaviors based on those thoughts. This trick, which
confuses thoughts with intentions or behaviors, is called *thought–action
fusion*. Thought–action fusion says that having thoughts about committing heinous acts makes it more likely that you'll commit them; it also says
that you're morally reprehensible for having such thoughts in the first
place, further heaping on feelings of guilt. Guilt is also common as a

reaction to the inconveniences that your symptoms may place on others. Even though no one would choose having OCD, our brains still love to twist the knife and try to convince us that our suffering is our own fault.

Anger or frustration may also rear up in the struggle to manage symptoms. Navigating the world with OCD can make you feel like you're constantly dodging land mines that don't appear to affect other people. So you not only have to contort your body and brain to avoid these triggers but also have to play it off so that no one else can tell. That's incredibly frustrating! And when a loved one steps squarely on the land mine that you so painstakingly avoided, it's often not going to be the only thing that explodes! We can't expect everyone to follow OCD's rules, and honestly, much of this book is about how asking others to do so only makes things worse because it perpetuates the cycle OCD depends on. But none of this makes your anger, irritation, exasperation, and rage any less valid or potent.

All these emotions, along with jealousy (the redheaded stepchild of the social emotions), can and do affect the friendships, partnerships, and other relationships of people with OCD. These emotions are likely often in the driver's seat when it comes to your decision making about relationships. Recognizing that emotions arise naturally as part of the human experience will help you take a step back from judging these natural occurrences and heaping on more discomfort. It's my hope that the activities in this book will help you change your automatic responses to them.

COGNITIVE BARRIERS

Our cognitions—or thoughts—help us make sense of the world and anticipate future events. They can alter our perception of the world, motivate our behaviors, and profoundly affect the emotions that we experience. But OCD commandeers this essential capability and turns the volume up sky high. "How about we try to make sense of things that philosophers have been debating for millennia?" says Existential OCD. "You're afraid about running someone over? Let's construct an alternate reality in which all pedestrians are highly likely to end up crushed under these wheels and then imagine it in painstaking detail!" says Harm OCD. When you have OCD, you may exalt your thoughts as the most important indicators of danger, uncertainty, and potential demise. However, the truth is that some thoughts are just mental flotsam that wash up on the shores of our brains from time to time. They need not be treated as indications of anything other than a brain just doing its thing—making connections and predictions about the world.

Many researchers have examined the thought patterns associated with OCD and have concluded that specific biases or *distortions* tend to pop up. These thinking styles can make OCD worse and often present a skewed view of reality. *Overestimation of risk* is a particularly pesky example. With this distortion, things are dangerous until proven safe, and sometimes gathering this "proof" of safety can be a fruitless task. In terms of relationships, which tend to have a lot of unpredictable moving parts, people with OCD may be reluctant to get involved, or they may, in the absence of any evidence, assume that a negative outcome is inevitable. This is an overestimation of risk in action. *Catastrophizing* is the overestimation-of-risk bias taken to its natural conclusion: things are not only probably unsafe but will lead to the worst-case scenario if left to progress naturally. Related to this is another distortion called *inflated responsibility*. People with inflated responsibility feel that it's their moral imperative to prevent any possible harm. This sounds lovely until you think of the repercussions of having such a bias: every action has a possible negative outcome: *Was my smile at my employee creepy? Do they feel weird now? Should I email them to check, or is that even creepier?* Inflated responsibility can make you question every action and believe that you have either caused harm or failed to prevent it.

Much has been written about OCD and uncertainty. In fact, some argue that at its core, OCD is based on *intolerance of uncertainty*. Most of us accept that there's some level of uncertainty, and therefore risk, in various activities that we do day to day. We ride at great speeds in metal death boxes (cars) down narrow concrete pathways (highways) and trust that we'll probably make it to our destinations unscathed. But when OCD attaches to a theme, it makes that tolerance for uncertainty plummet. If you have contamination concerns about asbestos, for example, then it suddenly doesn't matter if your spouse entering the house has a 90 percent or a 0.009 percent chance of having asbestos on her clothing; OCD still wants her to disrobe and take a shower. *Perfectionism* is a related distortion that can't accept anything less than 100 percent. Perfectionism can appear in all kinds of ways if you have OCD, but striving for perfection or trying to choose behaviors that will protect you against "failure" are two common examples that can interfere with relationships.

And just because OCD loves to be difficult, it often attacks your *metacognitions*, or thoughts about thoughts. These are the beliefs that we hold about our thoughts, like whether we perceive them as highly important or as trivial mental junk. Again, if you have OCD, chances are you're more likely to place a great deal of significance on your thoughts. You may also believe that worrying is a productive way to work toward solving your problems. Finally, with OCD you're more likely to believe that you can and should control your thoughts. Other people in your life may not understand why you choose to structure your behavior around threats that are entirely internal (*I had a thought about harming the baby, so I can't be alone with him*). If you tend to believe your thoughts because they feel so real, then you likely have this kind of common distortion about the importance of thoughts.

BEHAVIORAL BARRIERS

We've already touched on avoidance, perhaps the most impairing behavioral barrier with OCD. Avoidance can interfere at any stage of a relationship, but it can also prevent a relationship from happening altogether. For example, I worked with a young woman who had unwanted sexual thoughts about children. Despite longing to build a family, she refused to take the first step toward meeting a partner. She reasoned that it would be unfair to her future partner not to be able to give him a family, because she worried she would never be able to feel safe around kids. She avoided any social events in which she might meet someone attractive and "lead them on" without intending to have children with them. Her fears of harming others were strong enough to short-circuit her reasoning about the types of relationships available to her. With steady encouragement and exposure work, however, she was able to cultivate curiosity about others and find a partner. As a bonus, she was able to attend her boyfriend's nephew's bar mitzvah and be around dozens of kids, an act that pitted her values (love for her boyfriend) against OCD's fears (that she would harm a child). None of this would have been possible had she stayed on the path of avoidance.

Engaging in compulsions is another behavior that can prevent people with OCD from cultivating and thriving in relationships. These may be overt compulsive behaviors that interfere with the time that you invest in relationships or may be mental rituals that take you out of the moment with loved ones. One of my clients tearfully recounted an incident during which she spent hours working during a weekend while her housemates enjoyed a rare snowstorm in Nashville. They built a snowman and went sledding while she was inside, triple- and quadruple-checking a report. The following year, she was crestfallen but not surprised when her housemates moved into a new apartment together without her. In therapy, she was able to process how her compulsions prevented her from nurturing relationships that she desired, and she committed to changing her behavior to better align with her values.

Examining Your Own Barriers

Which barriers do you struggle with? Do strong emotions sidetrack you from your relational life? Are your thoughts a stumbling block to connecting with others? Do compulsions get in the way? Whatever your answers to these questions, I want you to know that it is possible to confront these barriers and overcome them, and your relationships with others can and will improve when you do.

To close this chapter, I want to give you an exercise to open you to the possibility of pursuing the connections you deserve. All you'll need is five minutes of uninterrupted time and a willingness to get curious about your thoughts. You might want to read through the exercise first and then try it out, or you can also listen to the audio recording available at http://www.newharbinger.com/50584.

You Too Deserve Connection:
A Self-Compassion Exercise

Find a quiet place where you can engage fully with this activity. Sit in a comfortable chair or lie down, whichever you prefer.

To begin, take a few deep breaths, observing the sensations of air passing through your nose and throat each time you breathe in and breathe out. Slow down and focus your attention on the rhythm: in and out, in and out. Imagine that the air is tinted your favorite color, so that you can visualize it flowing all the way to the bottom of your lungs, high-fiving the bottom, and returning out through your nose. If you're not feeling the color tint, be playful with the imagery that works for you: maybe imagine that the air is iridescent or made of soothing steam or comprising thousands of tiny kittens—find something that you can use to help focus on pulling your breath deep into your lungs and belly. Notice any thoughts that arise as you focus on the breath. They're reminders that our brains like to wander away from tasks. You may be thinking thoughts like *I'm not doing this right*. Or *I hate mindfulness*. Or *Lung kittens? Seriously?*

Notice your thoughts with gentleness and nonjudgment and then return to the anchor of your breath.

Now, if you're willing, think of something painful that arises when you imagine yourself in relationships. Think of a reason that you picked up this book. Maybe it's an event in the past, like a fight with a loved one about your symptoms. Maybe it's a distressing belief, like a stern voice telling you that you don't deserve a partner. Maybe it's a fear that lives in the future, like a worry about parenting with OCD.

Breathe.

Create some space for this thought. Recognize and label this thought as a moment of suffering. Let yourself be aware of how painful this is. Notice where it lives in your body. Is it tightening up your chest, or tugging at your windpipe? Label the emotions that come up, such as *I feel a sense of grief. I feel alone. I feel ashamed.* And tell yourself, *I notice that I'm in pain. I notice that this is really hard.*

Good job staying with this suffering. Now imagine that you're connected to everyone else reading this book at this moment and everyone else who has ever read this book in the past. Imagine that you're connected to every human who experiences OCD and every human who has experienced suffering—in other words, all of us. Acknowledge and honor this shared experience. Many others have had this same thought, this same image, or this same fear. Everybody suffers. Allow yourself to sink into the knowledge that you're not alone.

Still with me? Good. I know this is hard, but you're doing great.

Now imagine the face of someone you care about. It can be a friend, a partner, a parent, or a child. It can be someone you know very well or someone you want to know better. Imagine this person telling you that they have had the painful thought that you just had. What would you tell this lovely human? Talk to yourself as you would to this other person. Allow yourself to receive the love and support that you would give them. And if it's too difficult to step away from the critical mind, simply tell yourself that you're working toward being kind to yourself. You may say: *May I practice self-kindness. May I learn to love and accept myself as someone who deserves kindness. May I be patient with myself as I learn this.*

You can return to this exercise anytime you find yourself being critical about what you have to offer in relationships. In those moments, finding self-compassion will put you in a better place to foster the connections you deserve.

Moving Forward

As you walk away from this page and go on about your day, see if you can catch some of your self-critical thoughts midstream. Practice noticing them, reminding yourself of the common experience of suffering, and holding yourself gently and kindly. The next chapter will look at how relationships can sneakily contribute to the OCD cycle and at how your loved ones can be supportive in ways that truly uplift you and not your OCD.

CHAPTER 2

Accommodation and Reassurance
Your Relationships' Role
in Your OCD

Supportive relationships can make dealing with OCD less overwhelming and more empowering. Having someone in your corner at home, work, or school to listen to and validate your struggles can be the difference between suffering in silence and having allies on the path toward wellness. However, sometimes the very behaviors that seem most supportive end up feeding the OCD cycle and exacerbating symptoms. This happens when those around us knowingly or unknowingly participate in rituals or provide the temporary relief that OCD craves.

Imagine you're a parent in the checkout line at the grocery store with your five-year-old son in tow. You've both had a long day, and it's an hour past his usual dinnertime. As you approach the bright sea of candy and gum lining the aisle, your son reaches out for a handful of chocolate. "Can we get this?" Wide eyes look up at you, pleading. "No, we're not going to get any candy today," you tell him. "But I'm hungry!" he protests. "We'll eat dinner soon," you promise, and as soon as those words leave your mouth, a wail begins to issue from his downturned mouth. As the wail gets louder and louder, you notice others in the store glancing your way. You're faced with the choice that a thousand parents have faced in the past: whether to quell him with a brightly wrapped snack or endure his distress and the judgment of others. While it may make sense in the short term to end his suffering, it won't help your son learn that he can ride the wave of discomfort and come out on the other side of it. Also, it's almost guaranteed that the next time you're in the grocery, he'll cry for the candy even harder.

I'm not saying that having OCD magically transforms people into hungry preschoolers. However, if you've ever enlisted others in your compulsive quests for certainty or safety, you can probably identify at least a little with the child here. And if you've ever been asked for reassurance about an unknowable question ("Are you *sure* it's going to be okay?"), you have had the experience of the parent too—that it's easier to quell someone's suffering than to sit with their suffering.

We've all been on both sides of this story because interdependence is a part of the human experience. We want to soothe those we love, and doing so is part of how we show intimacy and care for one another. But when you have OCD, you may more frequently find yourself in the child's position—very hungry and sensing that your only access to the food you want is through the actions your loved ones take. You may also find that both you and your loved ones are exhausted by navigating these situations. This chapter will look at how your relationships and your loved ones may be influencing your OCD—just as much as your OCD influences those relationships—and what you can do about it.

How Others Accommodate Your OCD

Because we are social creatures, compulsive urges demand behavioral change not only for the person with OCD but also for the others in their orbit. Loved ones may adhere to OCD's rules; participate in rituals; avoid places, situations, items, or topics that provoke symptoms; change their schedules to work around compulsions; take on additional responsibilities; or provide excessive reassurance (Lebowitz, Panza, and Bloch 2016). They can also engage in compulsions-by-proxy, such as when friends or family members check, research, or clean to ensure that the person with OCD doesn't have to. In the treatment literature, this phenomenon of changing one's behaviors in response to a loved one's symptoms is called *symptom accommodation,* and it's nearly universal in the lives of people with OCD and anxiety. At least 90 percent of families affected by OCD say they accommodate (Wu et al. 2016). Many of us who work with OCD like to say, jokingly, that the other 10 percent are lying.

In my fifteen years of work with kids, teens, and adults with OCD, it's hard to think of anyone unaffected by symptom accommodation in at least one of their relationships: parents completing their children's homework to prevent them from getting stuck in rewriting rituals; spouses changing their clothes in a "staging area" to avoid bringing outside contamination into the home; friends doing all the driving to relieve their pal of confronting vivid hit-and-run imagery; or countless topics and phrases banned from conversations for fear of provoking OCD symptoms. It's a natural response for several reasons.

First, we want to protect the people we care about. That means that for your loved ones, providing you with immediate relief may feel like the compassionate way to approach an otherwise frustrating common enemy in OCD. Another possible reason is that the loved one who provides the accommodation also has anxiety, which gives them empathy for you. Unsurprisingly, parents with anxiety or OCD report higher levels of accommodating behaviors with their kids than parents without these mental health concerns (Kagan, Frank, and Kendall 2017). This makes sense, as many parents will tell you that the only thing tougher than enduring their own uncomfortable feelings is watching their children do so. Additionally, loved ones often report that resisting accommodation feels unkind. Kids whose parents reduce accommodation may say things like "If you loved me, you would open that door for me!" "You're a mean mommy!" And the pièce de résistance: "I hate you!"

Besides all of the above, accommodation may be a way for your loved ones to manage their own anxiety about your discomfort. That is, if loved ones watch you struggle with your anxiety, they have to manage their own emotions about seeing you struggle. Further, if this happens in a public place, they may want to minimize any conflict or attention placed on your symptoms. For example, if you're out to eat and about to ask the waiter to clean what appears to be a contaminated fork, your spouse may instead want to reveal the "safe" fork from home they brought along to avoid causing any troubles to others. This is more about your spouse avoiding their own social anxiety or discomfort than it is about helping. It may also be true that partners continue accommodating because reducing accommodation—at least in the moment that it's demanded—is rarely met with an expression of gratitude by the person whose OCD craves it. Finally, people who accommodate may worry about the outcomes for their loved one if they were to refrain from accommodating: *Will my wife fail to show up to work and lose her job if I don't help with her morning rituals? Will my teenager become so upset that he harms himself if I don't replenish the toilet paper every day?* These can feel like impossible choices in the moment.

Recognizing Negative Consequences

Given how prevalent accommodation is, it would be nice to say that it's just an innocuous way for people to show affection for their loved ones with OCD. But as you've probably surmised, the act of accommodating OCD symptoms has a negative impact on both parties in the relationship. Research consistently shows that symptom accommodation is associated with poorer treatment outcome and greater symptom severity for people with OCD (Lebowitz, Panza, and Bloch 2016). In fact, accommodation is in direct opposition to the goals of ERP and ACT, two evidence-based treatments for OCD (introduced in chapter 1). These treatments encourage you to confront difficult situations in a gradual manner that's also informed by the values you want to embody. This, in turn, can help you reclaim things that OCD has rendered inaccessible. Accommodation, on the other hand, does the opposite: helping you to avoid or circumvent difficult situations. With accommodation, you never learn that you can get through situations without the use of a compulsion or avoidance, which stifles your motivation to reach toward goals that your OCD says are impossible. Conversely, when accommodation is reduced during treatment, people tend to show correspondingly fewer symptoms, regardless of how severe their symptoms were to begin with.

High levels of accommodation are also associated with what health providers call *functional impairment*. This is a measure of how well you function in the major domains of living, such as work, school, family, and social life. When loved ones accommodate, they deprive you of the opportunity to continue expanding your world and to develop self-efficacy and independence. To draw the earlier comparison: while your kiddo in the grocery store is happy to get his candy each time, he also becomes more distressed and less able to function without it.

Finally, those who accommodate experience negative consequences as well. You may have already experienced this with significant people in your life expressing anger, confusion, or hopelessness while struggling to keep ahead of OCD's demands. Family accommodation is correlated with increased burden, stress, and resentment on the part of caregivers (Lee et al. 2015). Siblings who accommodate experience more stress and poorer mental health outcomes than those who do not (Kagan, Frank, and Kendall 2017). And accommodation also affects the quality of the relationship itself, resulting in higher levels of conflict and lower levels of family cohesion (Peris et al. 2012). (Most of the research about the impact of accommodation on loved ones has focused on family members of those with OCD, but it's likely that other relationships are similarly impacted.) Clearly, instead of improving the lives of those with OCD or their loved ones, accommodation is feeding the OCD itself. In his book, *When a Family Member Has OCD*, Jon Hershfield describes accommodation as making more space in the relationship for the OCD to proliferate (2015). It's essentially hanging up a banner and putting out a welcome mat for future symptoms.

Does this mean that every friend, coworker, partner, or family member should halt all accommodating behaviors at once? This is a great place to stop and recognize that, as with almost everything else in this book, it's not a simple all-or-nothing issue. With OCD, the accommodating behavior of those in your life has probably developed over months and even years. Taking that away in one fell swoop would likely feel cruel. Sharing your symptom information with others is already a difficult task, and having them no longer adapt around your symptoms may feel like an attack on the relationship itself. Therefore, the answer is more nuanced: while reducing accommodation is an ongoing goal, the pace and the content of these reductions look different for every relationship.

Even therapists accommodate, and for good reason! If I were to treat every client with the same behavior, regardless of symptoms, I would run the risk of driving folks straight out of my clinic. So, when a client lets me know that they would rather not shake hands or have an appointment at an even-numbered hour, I don't demand immediate change. If clients aren't ready to change their behavior, we make a note to challenge it in the future and work up to it. Just as every step counts with exposure therapy, so does every attempt to reduce the role of accommodation in relationships.

Identifying Accommodation in Your Relationships

Because OCD can easily become entangled in relationships, you may not be aware of the impact of symptom accommodation in your everyday life or what kinds of accommodation your OCD demands. The following list of common accommodations may be a good jumping-off point for assessing the role that accommodation plays in your relationships. As you browse the list, be sure to consider how these behaviors may impact multiple relationships in your life. Make notes in your journal and share your responses with loved ones. What you discover here will inform later work in this chapter.

Excessive reassurance seeking or needing to know: when others must answer questions, give affirmation, or provide nonverbal feedback to assuage uncomfortable feelings (for example, anxiety, insecurity, doubt, guilt, or shame); others must provide information that feels urgent or important to attain a "just right" feeling.

Scripting: when conversations with others must go a certain way; for example, demanding that "Good night" must always be followed by "I love you."

Verbal downloading: when others must listen to a verbal rundown of past events, the function being either to confess things that you feel you may have done wrong or to simply clear the mental slate.

Washing or cleaning: when others must maintain certain washing or cleaning behaviors in line with OCD's rules.

Checking: when others must check things excessively, either to relieve you of the responsibility of checking or to ensure that things are safe (or both).

Avoidance: when others must avoid people, places, things, or concepts that provoke your symptoms or to help you avoid things that trigger you.

Financial support of rituals: when others must purchase things to support your rituals (such as buying extra soap, toilet paper, or clothing).

Taking on extra responsibilities: when others must complete chores or other tasks that would normally fall to you but that provoke your symptoms.

Revising schedules or deadlines: when others must change their schedules, routines, or expectations of timely completion of tasks to make more time for you to complete rituals or to otherwise follow OCD's rules.

Altering availability: when others must be available for contact or to physically help at times dictated by your OCD.

You might have noticed that while some of these behaviors are clearly more compulsive, such as scripting or checking, others may manifest as exaggerated versions of typical behavior. For example, we all ask for and make concessions in our schedules to adapt to one another's needs. Recently, against all logic and in defiance of perfectly good gravity, my husband decided to pursue his pilot's license. While he's away at flight lessons in the evenings, I've taken on more household duties and reduced my activities outside of the house to be home with the dog. However, his choice to study aviation is one fueled by his values of lifelong learning and adventure. In contrast, the choices that OCD presents to us are usually choices of avoidance—trying to escape uncomfortable feelings, thoughts, sensations, or situations. If you're having trouble figuring out if something is an accommodation, don't worry—we're calling in some help from your social network!

Accommodation Assessment: *Starting the Conversation*

In this exercise, you'll have a conversation with a loved one who accommodates your OCD about the patterns the two of you have fallen into and how you might be able to break them at a pace that works well for both of you. You should do this activity jointly with a loved one who has been empathetic to your struggles with OCD and who has expressed a willingness to change their behavior.

You'll need to carve out at least twenty minutes without distractions to have a conversation. It's best to do this one-on-one, rather than with more than one person at a time, and to do it in real time instead of sending the questions out and waiting to receive answers. The exercise may bring up strong emotions as you listen to your loved one's responses. But know that you and your loved ones are on the same team with the common goal of learning how best to connect in the face of OCD's demands. Examples of accommodation aren't evidence of personal failure or moral weakness. In fact, clarifying them will help you and your loved one see the ways that OCD has affected both of you so that you can systematically reduce these behaviors over time. Bring a heaping dose of self-compassion, and let the following script and questions guide you.

Start with this statement: "Imagine that we both wake up tomorrow, and my OCD is gone. I no longer find myself in the grips of looping thoughts, repetitive behaviors, mental rituals, or avoidance. Think about how your behavior would change from that moment forward."

Then ask these questions, allowing plenty of time for your loved one to respond to each one. Be sure to jot down their answers in your journal:

★ What would you want to do that you don't do now?

★ How would your daily routine change?

★ What would you want us to do together?

★ How would your language with me change? Are there certain things we could talk about more freely?

★ How would you spend your time differently?

★ What would there be more of?

★ What would there be less of?

How did the conversation go? What did you learn from it? Was there anything you heard that could help you and your loved one make some changes?

Way to go! You had the tough conversation. You both united to shine a spotlight on some of the ways that OCD has rooted into the relationship. Later in this chapter, you'll use this information in building your accommodation-reduction hierarchy.

The Reassurance Trap

While accommodation can take many forms, providing reassurance is a uniquely common one that can be particularly tricky to tease apart (Halldorsson et al. 2016). Part of this is because reassurance is important in every relationship. We check in with our supervisors to ensure that we're fulfilling our duties at work. We ask for feedback from our partners as we navigate changes, such as opening up a relationship to polyamory or deciding whether or not to have children. There's usually a genuine desire to seek clarifying information in these instances and an openness to a variety of responses. Asking for reassurance isn't necessarily compulsive, but as someone with OCD, you'll probably want to get good at identifying when it is.

Reassurance seeking in the service of the OCD cycle tends to follow from a subjective feeling and a desire to reduce that feeling. It's generally an attempt to get a specific answer rather than to provide clarity. Additionally, it can feel like an insatiable urge, such that any reassuring statement you get from someone just leads to another what-if. Finally, the need for reassurance can lead you to demand absolute certainty in situations that are inherently uncertain. That is, while most of us are satisfied with a "probably" or even a "maybe," OCD demands an unequivocal yes or no. It even demands this from unqualified sources, such as when a ten-year-old client posted pictures of her tonsils on social media to allow her friends (quite likely not credentialed medical professionals, but I'm willing to accept the uncertainty) to reassure her about the absence of a strep infection. "Let me know in the comments!"

For another example of how seeking reassurance can feel like digging your way out of a hole with a shovel, consider the following dialogue between Chase, a thirty-two-year-old man with OCD, and his sister Tara.

Chase: Are you sure it's okay if I come to the barbecue today? I don't think I should be around the new baby. She's so little, and I've been coughing today.

Tara: You told me that you already went to the doctor and everything was fine. I'll see you at 5:00.

Chase: But it could be something more serious. It's not right for me to put your kids at risk.

Tara: You always have allergies this time of year, so I'm sure it's nothing.

Chase: But what if this time it's not allergies, and I have something really nasty?

Tara: I think if it was something concerning, you'd have more than just itchy eyes and a little cough.

Chase: But it could be the beginning of a respiratory infection that's contagious.

Tara: I'm okay with you taking that risk. Please come.

Chase: But if I come, and it's something worse, I might spread it. Then you'll feel awful because you told me to come, and I'll feel like it's my fault. I should just stay home in case...

From this conversation, it's clear that Chase's OCD will always have another question no matter what Tara tells him. His attempts to feel better about the choice have actually made the choice more confusing. This pattern is an OC-normal response to OCD's demands for 100 percent safety and certainty. Reassurance seeking can present as asking direct questions, or it can be sneakier. Sometimes it appears as a statement ("I should probably stay home") and sometimes it appears as a confession ("I went to the barbecue while I had a cough"). In both instances, there's often an expectant pause after the statement so that the other person can provide words of safety or certainty ("I'm sure it's fine").

Whenever I talk about this topic in support groups for family members, their hands shoot up with questions. "So you're telling me not to tell my child that I love her?" Not if telling her thirty times earlier that day hasn't assuaged her anxiety. "You're saying that I shouldn't let my brother know that his fear of me being a doppelgänger instead of his real sibling is unfounded?" I'm not saying that you have to agree or disagree with the worry; rather, treat it like the brain blip it is and come back to supporting your loved one by refocusing on something that won't spiral his symptoms out of control. And if you have OCD, I would say the same thing. As much as you might want others to do it, providing excessive reassurance is undoubtedly scratching the itch.

Building a Reassurance Tracking System

When I ask clients about how frequently they seek reassurance, they're often flummoxed. For some, reassurance seeking has become so automatic that it's hard to distinguish it from noncompulsive behavior. That's why it helps to have a reassurance tracking system. Having a system to track your reassurance is like keeping a food log for a dietitian. They need to see what we're working with before they can figure out what to tweak to help you meet your goals.

Building awareness of reassurance seeking can be the first step toward implementing response prevention, the RP part of ERP. As a reminder, response prevention involves resisting the compulsive urges that keep you stuck in the OCD loop. While exposure gets a lot of attention as the more exciting element of ERP, it's inadequate without response prevention. In fact, exposure alone can reinforce OCD symptoms, such as when someone with relationship OCD watches a movie featuring a divorce (as an exposure) and then seeks reassurance from their partner about the state of the relationship and union. Therefore, we'll begin with a reassurance tracking system as a first step in response prevention. Once you are aware of your reassurance seeking, you can work to gradually reduce the frequency of reassurance seeking over time.

Use the "Reassurance Tracking" worksheet available online at http://www.newharbinger.com/50584. First write down some situations where you asked for reassurance. Then answer the questions in the next set of columns: What emotions were you experiencing? Did you ask only once? Was the source credible? Did you accept their response? These questions can be helpful in tracking how reassurance manifests for you. If you have uncomfortable feelings like anxiety, fear, doubt, or disgust, it's more likely that the behavior is functioning to reduce discomfort and is compulsive. If you asked for reassurance more than once or in different ways, that's another hint that OCD is at play. The credible-source question can help you consider whether this was an appropriate person to ask. As previously mentioned, OCD often just wants you to feel *better*, not truly informed. So when you accept answers from unqualified sources, this may be another indicator that what you're doing is a compulsive action. Finally, consider whether you were able to accept the answer provided. Did you ask someone else? Did you check the internet? Your responses to these questions may be clues to whether OCD is ramping up.

Filling out this worksheet will help you recognize if what you are doing is reassurance seeking (a symptom of OCD) or information seeking (not a symptom of OCD). However, this is not meant to be a test to see if your actions are compulsive (treating it as a test could—surprise!—become a compulsion itself) but to help you consider the factors that play into your style of reassurance seeking. Here are two possible responses to the worksheet questions; note that in the second example, not all indicators of OCD were present, even though these were compulsive behaviors.

Example 1

Situation: Asked my partner about a weird bump on my leg

What were your emotions? Anxiety, dread

Asked once? No

Credible source? No

Accepted answer? No

Example 2

Situation: Asked my friend if she was mad at me

What were your emotions? Anxiety

Asked once? No

Credible source? Yes

Accepted answer? No

While the goal of this worksheet is initially just to track symptoms—rather than attempt to reduce them—you may find yourself refraining from asking for reassurance because you don't want to have to write it down (kind of like someone with a low-sodium diet magically eating fewer frozen meals when asked to track their intake). But the main goal of the worksheet is to build awareness. With greater awareness of when and how reassurance tends to pop up in your relationships, you may find yourself more likely to resist these urges and sit in the uncertainty. And maybe, just maybe, you can see yourself coming out on the other side of those urges.

Reducing Accommodation as Exposure Therapy

Reducing accommodation can be hard for both the person providing it and the person receiving it. The good news is that doing so is a form of exposure therapy that ultimately benefits both parties.

Lori and Tasha's Story

Lori and Tasha had already been best friends for over ten years by the time I started working with Lori. They met in early high school as competitive swimmers who trained with the same coach. After graduating, both worked part-time as swim instructors at their old gym. While Tasha attained her bachelor's degree and eventually became a full-time assistant trainer, Lori continued to work with the youngest children at the pool a few days per week. She enrolled in community college classes a few times but was able to complete only one per semester. Moreover, she continued to live with her mother while her peers found apartments and became more independent. She reported feeling stuck and hopeless in her current situation but noted that Tasha was one of her biggest supports.

Lori met criteria for severe OCD, with symptoms centering around themes of harm and religious scrupulosity. She experienced vivid images of herself veering into oncoming traffic or holding her students underwater to drown them. Moreover, she experienced doubt about using inappropriate touch while guiding the children through their skills and worried whether she was a faithful Christian worthy of salvation. Most of Lori's compulsions consisted of repeating behaviors over and over until she attained the feeling that these feared consequences wouldn't or hadn't come true. They took up hours of her day. She also avoided situations that could lead to harm, such as driving alone or using knives.

Tasha, who valued loyalty above all else and who knew Lori before her OCD symptoms appeared in late adolescence, longed to see Lori living her life to the fullest. To this end, she often shifted her work schedule to match Lori's so she could follow her home and provide reassurance that Lori hadn't hit anyone. Sometimes she would wait upwards of thirty minutes at the gym for Lori to finish her rituals before the drive home. Moreover, she wanted to support Lori's faith, which had been a way they had bonded as teens. After a few failed attempts to have Lori join for worship at Tasha's church, Tasha decided that she would travel to Lori's house on Sunday mornings so that they could worship together, since this was the only way that was available to Lori. She did this at the expense of attending her own church but rationalized that she was still able to attend Wednesday evening services, at least on the days that she wasn't helping Lori drive home.

I felt a tremendous amount of compassion for both young women. Lori had lost years to her OCD and reported that she felt developmentally stunted by her symptoms. She cited Tasha as part of *the reason that she was able to keep her job and remain tied to her faith. Tasha believed that she was doing everything possible to help Lori live a life outside of her OCD. However, a frank assessment of the situation helped everyone see that Tasha's accommodating behaviors were helping Lori remain stuck. They helped her to just barely cling to a job that was less than fulfilling and prevented her from getting the more intensive care that she needed to address her symptoms. Shortly after our work together began, Lori took a leave from work to complete a day treatment program for her symptoms. There she practiced driving independently, watching church services online, and learning assertiveness skills to use upon her return to work. The relationship between Tasha and Lori evolved from one of enabling to one of mutual contribution and respect. Tasha sometimes felt guilty when she set limits with Lori, but she worked through this with her own therapist.*

A good way to address reducing accommodation is through creating an exposure hierarchy, because doing this allows you to ease into the process, starting with the least difficult exposure and working your way up. Consider the chart below with an example from Lori and Tasha's story. Note that in this exposure hierarchy, you list the accommodations that you plan to reduce in order from least to most difficult ("Tasha follows me only halfway home" comes before "Tasha doesn't follow me home" and so on). Next you rate these actions on a 1 to 10 scale in terms of your willingness to try them out, where 1 means completely unwilling and 10 means completely willing. After you've created your list and rated your willingness, your loved one can use the same scale to rate their own willingness. You can then mutually decide on target dates for achieving each reduction in accommodation. This will help you to build a plan to gradually reduce these behaviors and over time expand your world and confidence.

Accommodation Reduction	Your willingness/ your loved one's willingness (1 to 10 scale)	Target date
Tasha follows me only halfway home from work	8 / 10	Now
Tasha doesn't follow me home from work	5 / 8	1 month
Tasha stops coming over for Sunday worship	5 / 3	5 weeks

Now it's your turn to work on this with your own partner. First refer back to the list of common accommodations that you browsed earlier in this chapter, along with any journal notes about how these behaviors may impact your relationships, and review your loved one's responses in the accommodation assessment exercise. Then use the "Reducing Accommodations Hierarchy" available online at http://www.newharbinger.com /50584 to reduce your own accommodations. And get started!

Finding the Right Support for You (Not Your OCD)

It can be hard to recognize that the behaviors of loved ones that feel most encouraging may be keeping you stuck. But the good news is that, in making changes to how your loved ones accommodate you, all of you get a chance to come together for change. Your loved ones get to participate—by not participating in symptoms! We'll build on this concept throughout the remaining chapters as we help you to enlist others in reducing your symptoms and increasing your connectedness. Next, we'll explore a few of the symptoms that can be particularly hard on relationships.

CHAPTER 3

"I Can't See You Anymore"
OCD Subtypes That Center on Relationships

There's a phrase that we OCD therapists often utter: "It's not about the content." This means that regardless of the flavor of your symptoms—be they a soufflé of moral scrupulosity with a drizzle of checking, a casserole of just right and symmetry concerns, or a smorgasbord of assorted content areas—all forms of OCD follow the same pattern. There are uncomfortable thoughts, images, sensations, or impulses accompanied by mental or physical behaviors that serve to reduce this discomfort: same recipe, different ingredients. Therefore, in all these cases, we treat the symptoms identically, reducing compulsions and avoidance while increasing engagement with valued areas of life. We don't fall into the trap of ascribing significance to the themes themselves. In fact, focusing on the content can be your first step toward engaging in a compulsion. So instead of trying to figure out what your symptoms mean, it's often better to think of them like gnats buzzing around you. You wouldn't try to decipher any meaning in the gnats' flight patterns or the volume of their buzzing. You would just see them as annoyances whose presence need not control your behavior.

Similarly, any OCD theme can affect your relationships with others. However, certain subtypes of OCD are relational in nature; that is, if your symptoms reflect one of these subtypes—relationship OCD (ROCD), sexual orientation OCD (SO-OCD), gender-related OCD, or harm OCD—the content of your obsessions and compulsions will focus on your interactions with others. These symptom subtypes often lead to conflict and hamper your ability to be fully and genuinely intimate with others in relationships. In this chapter, we'll look at these subtypes more closely, explore how they can affect your life, and present skills to give you distance between your urges and the behaviors that you choose in your relationships.

Julio's Story

During Julio's first therapy session, he stated sheepishly that many of his worries centered on his wife, Maritza, and his ten-year-old daughter, Ana, both of whom he was quick to clarify he loved very much. However, he was plagued by intrusive images of his wife being intimate with past partners and felt compelled to compare these images to his own sexual intimacy with her. Moreover, he asked Maritza repeatedly if she intended to leave him for one of these partners and scrutinized her appearance to see if he was "well matched" with her in their levels of attractiveness. Julio asked others about this as well, imploring them to give ratings of his and Maritza's appearance on a scale of 1 to 10. When the numbers differed, Julio felt despondent and certain that the relationship was doomed to fail. Understandably, Maritza was exhausted by these behaviors and interpreted Julio's doubts as a lack of trust in her and a lack of faith in the relationship itself.

More difficult for the family, however, was Julio's tendency to fret over his daughter's intellectual abilities. Although Ana was well liked by peers and received As and Bs in her classes at school, Julio worried that she was falling behind both socially and academically. He scrutinized her behavior with playmates and often questioned his wife about her perceptions of Ana's abilities. These fears persisted despite other adults in Ana's life reporting no concerns. Julio advocated for Ana to receive educational testing when she was in second grade to rule out any learning issues. The testing revealed overall average intellectual functioning with no concerning areas of weakness, but Julio wondered if the results were a fluke. He wanted her to be retested the next year in case they had missed something, but the school wouldn't allow it. When he discussed this with his wife, she became angry. "You read over her homework like a hawk and scold her for minor errors in her grammar. She's just a child, and you're giving her a complex!" Julio felt ashamed about his behavior but also worried that if he didn't act, she would continue to fall behind. Both parents were relieved to hear that there was a name for Julio's symptoms: relationship OCD.

Coping with Relationship OCD

People with relationship OCD worry about significant people and relationships in their lives and attempt to reduce those worries with compulsions. Although the most common presentation of ROCD focuses on romantic partnerships, any significant relationship can become the target of symptoms, including friendships, parent–child relationships, or relationships at work.

ROCD can be difficult to identify because the content is highly relatable. Even in secure relationships between people with minimal anxiety, there's often some degree of checking in with one another about the status of the relationship or providing constructive feedback about behaviors. In that way, ROCD often lacks the unusual or taboo content of some other types of OCD and can therefore fly under the radar. However, for those suffering from ROCD, such worries about relationships are persistent and distressing. In other words, these ROCD gnats are plentiful and come equipped with tiny little megaphones to amplify their message. It's an all-caps swarm of THIS FRIENDSHIP IS DOOMED or MY HUSBAND ISN'T ATHLETIC ENOUGH.

As with all other themes of OCD, compulsions contribute to the loudness of the worries. Common compulsions in ROCD include reassurance seeking, checking, researching, comparing, rumination, and mental reviewing. People with ROCD may scrutinize their internal sensations to look for feelings of affection, romantic love, or sexual arousal to try to prove that they care enough about their loved one. They may go through their partners' phones or social media looking for evidence of infidelity. They may spend hours ruminating about past events and comparing them with current experiences with others, or seeking reassurance that they're a good friend, parent, child, or employee.

Just because ROCD has more pedestrian content than other OCD subtypes doesn't mean that it's any less painful or impactful. With ROCD, there are two main types of symptoms: those that focus on your relationships (relationship-centered ROCD) and those that focus on your loved ones (partner-focused ROCD).

Relationship-Centered ROCD

Relationship-centered ROCD is characterized by doubt, worry, and the scrutiny of significant relationships. Concerns may include the long-term viability of your relationship, your feelings toward a loved one, your loved one's feelings toward you, and the compatibility of the relationship (Doron et al. 2012). Julio's obsessions and compulsions that focused on his wife, Maritza, fall into this category.

It's also worth noting that although most narratives about romantic ROCD concentrate on monogamous relationships, people who practice ethical nonmonogamy may experience ROCD as well. For polyamorous people, the questions may be less about if a partner is *the one* and more about if a partnership fits into their current constellation of relationships or whether a partner's characteristics indicate that they'll be a good, loving, or appropriate person with whom to develop intimacy.

Partner-Focused ROCD

Partner-focused ROCD involves a preoccupation with perceived deficits a loved one has, such as their appearance, intelligence, morality, or personality characteristics (Melli et al. 2018). The loved one does not have to be a partner either. For example, Julio's concerns about his daughter Ana's social skills and academic abilities fall into partner-focused ROCD. While some partner-focused ROCD symptoms can resemble cruel indictments of loved ones, people who have these symptoms regret thinking these things. They may say, "I know he's a wonderful partner, but can I tolerate that weird laugh for the rest of my life?" or "I should love her regardless of her unibrow, but I can't stop thinking about it." Remember that this is one of OCD's oldest tricks, trying to convince you that the content of your obsessive thoughts says something about your character. However, all it truly says is that the relationship which OCD has wiggled its way into is very important to you.

Desperately Seeking Certainty

As much as we might like it to be otherwise, compatibility in relationships is never a sure thing. We have dating sites that pair up people based on personality factors, we may consult with religious or spiritual authorities to evaluate matches, or we may look to astrology to assist with cosmic connections. But try as we might, there's no foolproof way to measure the rightness of a relationship. In fact, even those of us who are thrilled with our relationships would be hard pressed to objectively measure and quantify our love (though such a test would be great fodder for a reality TV show). And considering the size of the world population, the odds suggest that as you gaze into your sweetie's eyes, there is someone, probably a hundred thousand someones, who may be better suited for you.

While this can seem terribly unromantic at first, the romance lies in the fact that two people have chosen to forge a relationship with one another despite the inevitable mismatched qualities and resulting bumps in the road. The work of maintaining relationships and friendships is an active exercise in choosing love: it's tolerating uncertainty and saying "I'm still here."

ROCD, like all OCD, isn't a fan of this uncertainty business. It wants to know without a shadow of a doubt that things are perfectly aligned, and this drive feels not like a curious question but like a necessary condition to continue engaging in the relationship. It almost becomes a moral dilemma: *How can I possibly go on with this if I don't know for sure? Am I leading this person on?* And because we can't quantify things like interpersonal connectedness or intimacy, knowing for sure is an impossible task. Therefore, for people with ROCD, the goal is to shift from knowing that a relationship's right (or that someone is good enough, that they love you enough, and so on) to accepting that right now, in this moment, it's worth trying to make it work or worth accepting your loved one as they are.

ROCD not only comes with a demand for certainty but also tells you that your worries need to be resolved urgently. You may think, *Not only do I need to know for sure, but I need to know now!* Again, there are cultural factors that can fuel these fears, especially for romantic relationships. We're often told that there's a timeline for major life events such as partnership, marriage, and having children, and we're given benchmarks for progress in other relationships as well. ROCD claims that if we aren't meeting those arbitrary deadlines, we're failing ourselves and our loved ones. This urgency can feel uncomfortable in the body: heart racing, chest tightness, and other panicky sensations. It can sound like worries that you'll waste years of your life, that you'll fail to help someone address their flaws, or that you'll be stuck in this tangle of anxiety with them forever.

Despite the persuasive tricks of ROCD, your challenge is to respond to these fears with a great big "maybe" and come back to being a partner, friend, or family member in the here and now—accepting that you can't perfectly control all outcomes in life or in your relationship but that you do have the ability to decide what you'll do here and now. Finally, combatting ROCD isn't about attributing all your relationship fears to OCD and therefore discounting them—this would just be a backdoor way to attain certainty. Treatment involves carrying out the behaviors that you value without knowing for sure. It's about accepting that after you drop the compulsions, you may still decide that the relationship's not worth pursuing. But at least you'll be the one making that decision, not your OCD.

Working on Response Prevention

You may be thinking that to do ERP for ROCD will mean brutal exposures to your worst fears: maybe writing scripts about never feeling 100 percent comfortable in your relationship or maybe scrutinizing your loved one's flaws ad nauseum. But that's not what we're going to do here. People with ROCD already tend to mentally drag themselves through the mud trying to prepare for the worst, so the real work is in disrupting that process through response prevention and moving on, even though your certainty itch hasn't been scratched.

Still, response prevention can be particularly difficult with ROCD given what we discussed earlier: oftentimes your symptoms can seem justifiable as typical behaviors or necessary to ensure the success of the relationship. You may be tempted to tell yourself, *Doing a little bit of research won't hurt* or *I really need to know if my friend cares about me this time.* Therefore, having a few solid statements to help you resist these urges can be the difference between feeding or fighting OCD. And you can use this technique for any OCD symptoms, not just ROCD ones.

Disrupting the Process: *Compulsion-Resistance Statements*

Use the following prompts to generate your own compulsion-resistance statements.

1. Think about what's most important to you when OCD is not the loudest voice in your mind. How does OCD prevent you from engaging with these important areas of your life? Example response: *I love family but spend less time with them because of intrusive incestuous thoughts.* How does it twist something important into an unhelpful behavior? Example response: *I strive to be organized, but my OCD blows this out of proportion and wants everything just so.* Now let's work on changing these responses into motivational statements. For example, you might say something like, "I'm striving to be able to spend time with my family with or without anxiety" or "I can be organized without having to be perfect."

2. Think of a past success when you confronted your fears or tolerated difficult emotions. For example, a woman with health-related compulsions was able to remind herself that when she had unexpected complications during childbirth, she was more physically and emotionally resilient than she would have predicted. Therefore, her compulsion-resistance statement was "I've proven to myself that I'm resilient. Even if the worst-case scenario happens, I'll get through it."

3. If you've been thinking a lot about how your symptoms must adversely affect others, turn this around with a positive statement: think instead about how your moments of discomfort in resisting a compulsion will positively impact others. This could sound like "My bedtime checking routine takes me away from quality time with my spouse, and I want this time back."

4. Remind yourself that the process of fighting OCD requires you to feel strong negative emotions along the way. No one loves being

itchy! Using statements to remind yourself that the discomfort is an effective component of the treatment can make you feel good about feeling bad. For example, you might say, "Just like with a muscle, the pain means it's making me stronger," "I'll choose to welcome discomfort as it means I'm hitting OCD where it hurts," and even "Bring it on!"

Write down the compulsion-resistance statements that you've created, and then use them as a wedge between your fear and your response.

Cultivating and maintaining relationships can be challenging when you have ROCD, but it's manageable when you're aware of the symptoms and proactive about challenging them. Armed with an acceptance for uncertainty and your compulsion-resistance statements, you can begin engaging with your partners, friends, and family from a place of connectedness instead of fear.

Sexual Orientation OCD and Gender-Related OCD

As with ROCD, the content of your obsessions and compulsions focuses on your interactions with others when you have sexual orientation OCD or gender-related OCD. With these two themes, however, the OCD symptoms attack your sense of identity.

Hannah's Story

Hannah had always considered herself to be very self-aware. She was an outspoken child who came out as a lesbian to her family and friends at age eleven. Her senior year of high school, she served as president of the school's gay–straight alliance club, spreading awareness about LGBTQIA+ issues and fighting for queer sexual

health topics to be covered in her school's wellness curriculum. She
intended to continue her advocacy work in college but stopped in her
first semester after reading an article written by a woman calling
herself a former lesbian. Hannah read the article with curiosity and
related somewhat to the author. They both shared an interest in
travel, came out before puberty, and endorsed a strong commitment to
social equality.

The thought occurred to her, What if I'm not really gay? *Hannah initially dismissed the thought, turning her attention to her girlfriend of thirteen months—a veritable marriage-length relationship in teenage terms. But secretly, she began researching coming-out stories to see how her own experience of exploring her sexual identity compared with others:* Had she given herself enough time to fully know her preferences? Was she mistaking friendship for romantic feelings? *Further, she began noticing a strange sensation of arousal around her male peers.* Had she not noticed this before? What did it mean? *And further, if she was straight, did that mean that she was a fraud in her community? By the time she arrived in therapy for OCD six months later, Hannah was stuck in endless rituals trying to get to the bottom of this question, including having broken up with her girlfriend to* "test out" *sexual intimacy with male classmates. She was miserable, exhausted, and further than ever from figuring it out.*

Hannah's symptoms are typical of sexual orientation OCD, a subtype in which people doubt their sexual orientation and seek certainty. In the past, this was sometimes called HOCD, or homosexual OCD, a label that was unnecessarily stigmatizing to people in the LGBTQIA+ community. Also, the term wasn't an accurate description, because it suggested that only heterosexual individuals experience these symptoms. Actually, as illustrated with Hannah's story, SO-OCD can occur across the spectrum of sexual orientations. Straight people can worry about being bisexual, asexual people can worry about being sexual, pansexual people can worry about being straight, and so forth.

Anyone can be affected by SO-OCD regardless of their personally held beliefs about sexuality and sexual orientation. That is, SO-OCD isn't a sign of homophobia or prejudice, although having negative beliefs about certain sexual orientations can certainly complicate the presence of SO-OCD symptoms. Moreover, given the negative stereotypes and stigma associated with sexual minorities, it's likely that we all have some level of negative bias, even if unconscious, in this area (Pinciotti et al. 2022). I bring this up because sometimes OCD latches onto this as another subject of desired certainty: *Am I homophobic or not?* Said another way, it's possible to have SO-OCD and not have any overt prejudices, but given that we are all steeped in a heterosexist culture, OCD can do a darn good job of using internalized homophobia against us.

Common rituals with SO-OCD include checking for sexual arousal, researching different orientations, reassurance seeking, mentally reviewing past interactions, mentally projecting possible future situations, and avoiding things that provoke unwanted thoughts. Studies show that SO-OCD is a common subtype, with between 10 and 25 percent of people with OCD having experienced this subtype at some point (Williams et al. 2015).

Kurtis's Story

Kurtis didn't think about gender for most of his life. He lived in a rural community where his exposure to gender-nonconforming people was limited. However, when he moved to Nashville for a job in his mid-thirties, he learned more about the transgender community. His neighbors were raising a transgender boy whose name and appearance were initially hard for him to reconcile. His company outlined progressive policies for the use of pronouns in all introductions and assured the availability of gender-inclusive restrooms in their offices. Up to this point, Kurtis's OCD symptoms had focused on contamination and existential themes, so when he first began to experience looping doubts about his own gender identity, he didn't recognize them as potentially obsessive.

As a child and teenager, Kurtis's penchant for cooking and a lack of interest in sports were the punchlines of jokes meant to poke at his masculinity. Although he brushed them off, later in his thirties these memories returned to him as possible evidence that he was transgender and in denial. It wasn't that he felt a true discrepancy between the gender he was assigned at birth and his true identity; rather, he found himself stuck in a series of what-ifs with no clear answer: What if I've always been a girl and just never knew it? What if I feel like I have to transition? What if have to tell my family and friends that I've been living a lie? *He scrutinized his interactions with friends of different genders and felt concerned when he was more comfortable with female friends. He was terrified about how his family and friends from home would react if he were trans, and he compulsively rehearsed how he might respond to their imaginary criticisms. Meanwhile, he found that his relationships with others were suffering as he spent more and more time in his head.*

Kurtis's symptoms are typical of gender-related OCD, which presents as urges to clarify your gender and concerns that such a fixation means your gender must differ from the one that you have lived in. Gender-related OCD has sometimes been referred to as trans OCD or TOCD in the literature, which suggests that only cisgender people (those whose gender matches the one assigned at birth) experience intrusive thoughts about being transgender. However, people of all gender identities can have gender-related OCD symptoms, which, for transgender people (those whose gender identity differs from that assigned at birth) may manifest as concerns about being cisgender or worries that they're "faking" their gender.

Common compulsions in gender-related OCD include comparing yourself with others who represent alternative gender identities, assessing yourself for "masculine" and "feminine" preferences or characteristics, researching gender identity, and checking for internal cues about whether your gender feels correct. For both SO-OCD and gender-related OCD, ERP and ACT are appropriate interventions. Exercises from both are woven throughout this book.

Looking for Authenticity

Imagine waking up one day to a loud knock on your door. When you go out, you see your mother standing on the stoop beside an unfamiliar woman. Your mother nervously smiles and asks if they can both come in. You invite them into your house, and the other woman introduces herself with a shaky voice. "Hello," she says with a smile. "I know this comes as a shock, but I'm your real mother." Your mother, or the person you assumed was your mother, begins to sob and verifies this. She tells you that your biological mother gave you up at birth to another family who had more resources to raise you. You think back on your childhood memories and begin to question them. You compare the faces of these two women and see the truth written all over your biological mother's features. An internal voice cries out: *I'm not who I thought I was. I've been living a lie.*

Both SO-OCD and gender-related OCD focus on the possibility that one day you will hear an internal voice telling you that you've been living a lie, a day when you realize that you've been duped. It's a worry about being duped by yourself rather than someone else—that *you* have accidentally gotten yourself all wrong. Your symptoms focus on the desire to live an authentic life and to align your actions with this authenticity. Many of the consequences of transitioning to a new sexuality or gender are relational in nature, including ending romantic and sexual relationships, navigating new communities or leaving old ones, facing social ostracism, or realigning your life with a newfound sense of self. Because any of these outcomes would upend your social world, sexuality and gender are natural targets for OCD.

While wanting to live authentically is an understandable goal, the very nature of OCD makes this feel like an impossible task. Attempts to verify your sexual orientation or gender identity invariably lead to more rather than fewer doubts. To make matters worse, many people with these subtypes of OCD experience strong physical sensations not so subtly called *groinal sensations* or *groinals*. These are unexpected feelings of arousal that you notice when evaluating your body for pleasure. They can take the form of erections, increased lubrication, feelings of warmth or flushness, or any perceived change in erogenous areas. Groinals can seem like compelling evidence of your attraction to others and can be misinterpreted as a more authentic signal of your sexuality than thoughts alone: *If I experience a groinal while hanging out with my male friends, am I gay?* They can get tangled up in gender identity too: *If I experience a groinal while hanging out with my male friends, am I a transgender woman living as a cisgender man?* The truth is that our bodies experience all kinds of sensations, and focusing attention on our genitals is likely to stir things up there. Chapter 6 about OCD and sex will return to this topic.

Flip-Flopping Between Avoidance and Compulsions

A tricky thing can happen with OCD that is particularly common with SO-OCD and gender-related OCD: the same behavior can switch between being an exposure and being a compulsion. Remember—exposure as a therapy means deliberately engaging in thoughts, feelings, behaviors, or sensations that increase your anxiety, or that OCD tells you to avoid, so that you can experience tolerating your anxiety. Compulsions, on the other hand, fulfill the opposite purpose: they're the things that you do to alleviate anxiety. But given that nothing's ever simple with OCD, the behaviors that you avoid can become compulsive, and compulsive behaviors can become feared ones that you avoid. Take, for example, pornography use in the context of SO-OCD. If as a heterosexual you worry about being gay, you may avoid watching same-sex porn for fear you'll become aroused, or, at other times, you may compulsively watch same-sex porn to check for sensations to evaluate how much you like it relative to straight porn.

This flip-flopping dance between avoidance and compulsive engagement can be dizzying and illustrates why it's important to focus on the function of the behavior as opposed to the behavior itself. Again, the truth is that your compulsions—even the ones that feel grueling and never ending—do perform some function in your life. They can provide relief and make you feel like you've done something for the obsessive thoughts and fears you're grappling with. However, they can also be damaging in the long term; the relief you get after doing a compulsion is only temporary, and engaging in compulsions makes the obsessive thoughts you have stronger, not weaker. This next exercise will help you differentiate between potential exposures and compulsive behaviors so you can get a clear sense of what you might want to try doing and what behaviors to resist.

Exposure or Compulsion: *Telling Them Apart*

Get out of sheet of paper and fold it in half. On one side write the word "Exposures" and on the other side write the word "Compulsions." Then ask yourself the following questions to help generate a list of possible exposures:

What kinds of situations, people, or behaviors trigger my fears?

What do I avoid because of my symptoms?

What might I be doing differently if I didn't have this kind of OCD?

What kinds of situations, people, or behaviors do I endure with distress because of my symptoms?

Write your answers in the exposures column. Then ask yourself the following questions to generate a list of compulsions:

What kinds of behaviors do I engage in to attain certainty about my sexual orientation or gender identity?

What kinds of thinking loops do I get stuck in when my OCD is triggered in this area?

What kinds of things do I have to do in a particular order or a very specific way because of these fears?

Write your answers in the compulsions column. When you're done, you'll have a list of things that can be possible exposures and a list of compulsions to resist. In concert with the other activities in this book, you'll be able to implement ERP for these difficult symptoms.

Make sure that you check back in with this list periodically to ensure that your exposures and compulsions haven't switched functions (and therefore columns) on you! If a behavior that you listed as an exposure ends up providing relief or reassurance, for example, it may need to switch columns. Or if a compulsive behavior feels suddenly scary to complete, you may want to consider recategorizing it as an exposure.

Harm OCD

Harm OCD is a subtype that consists of unwanted thoughts, images, impulses, or urges associated with harming others. It belongs in this chapter because like the other subtypes discussed here, harm OCD focuses on your interactions with others.

Miriam's Story

The first time that Miriam experienced a violent intrusive thought, she was sitting in synagogue listening to a service about forgiveness. The congregant directly in front of her was biting her nails and spitting little crescents of fingernail between the pews. Miriam looked at the soft spot at the nape of this woman's neck and imagined driving the tip of her car keys deep into the flesh there. She knit her hands

together and shuffled her purse to the right, avoiding the reflection
coming off her keys inside.

Later Miriam's violent thoughts began spreading to other
contexts, including unwanted thoughts of hitting pedestrians with her
car, poisoning her cat, and even sexually assaulting her toddler. She
resisted telling anyone about these thoughts for fear that they would
consider her dangerous or even take her child away. But Miriam
wasn't a dangerous person at all. She suffered from harm OCD.

Intrusive thoughts are so called because they intrude into your consciousness without your permission. Research shows that they're common
whether or not you have OCD, but those with OCD experience intrusive
thoughts more frequently and find them more distressing than those
without OCD (Bouvard et al. 2017). There are multiple potential reasons
for this, but recall that there are certain types of beliefs that people with
OCD tend to endorse at higher levels than those without it. Some of
these, like beliefs about the importance of thoughts, may make you feel
like having intrusive harm thoughts reveals something sinister about your
character and puts others around you at risk. If you believe that your
thoughts reveal something about your propensity to harm others, of
course you would do anything to get relief from them.

Violent obsessions are especially frequent for people with harm OCD
after just having or adopting children; parents often report an uptick in
images of harming their little ones either accidentally or on purpose. This
could be related to another common belief or feeling that people with
OCD report, the feeling of inflated responsibility. Because having a baby
truly does put you in a position of responsibility for a vulnerable life, OCD
can turn the volume up on harm thoughts. It's taking advantage of your
responsibility for another person and demanding that you prove yourself
to be fit for the job. You might think, *Would a good parent have these*
thoughts? Should I even be allowed to be alone with my children? Having
violent thoughts is understandably incredibly jarring, not because you
want to do the things that they represent but because you don't! And it's

also common in harm OCD to have thoughts about emotionally harming others.

Common compulsions for harm OCD consist of the usual suspects—avoidance (of sharp objects, vulnerable people, driving); checking to make sure you didn't harm someone; reassurance seeking; washing (to prevent contaminating someone else)—and boatloads of mental rituals. The latter often consist of various forms of self-assurance: reminding yourself that you would never do such things and that you find these thoughts abhorrent. But in true OCD style, your brain may argue back with you and try to convince you that you *did* want to have those thoughts or *would* consider hurting others. This is why it's important to drop the rope in your tug-of-war with OCD: it will always pull back. In addition to these compulsions, many people with harm OCD isolate themselves from others. The one-two punch of fearing that you might harm someone and being ashamed of these thoughts can make it feel like you don't deserve to be around others. This is perhaps the most damaging of the harm OCD compulsions when it comes to relationships.

Labeling Thoughts as Good or Bad

Absolute terms like "good" and "bad" can be harmful when you have an OC-normal brain. As soon as you call yourself good, you render yourself vulnerable to being knocked off that pedestal by any less-than-good action. With a perfectionistic brain, you can get paralyzed by knowing that although you're mostly good, you could certainly be better, so why aren't you trying harder? Labeling thoughts as good or bad is problematic too. Really, thoughts are just a collection of sounds strung together into a series of words. Equating having an intrusive thought with doing the act it suggests gives thoughts way more power than they deserve. In fact, to someone who doesn't speak this language, the sentence "I'm going to assault a child" would mean nothing at all. It's just gibberish.

Once you know that harm thoughts aren't meaningful, you can change your behavior around them. Intrusive thoughts are no longer a mandate to act, and resisting compulsions becomes more accessible. If you're still not convinced, consider this: people with OCD are no more likely—and are probably less likely—to commit the heinous things that pop into their minds than anyone else. Think of it this way: if you were truly a nefarious person, you would not spend your time trying to rid yourself of harm thoughts but would take delight in them instead.

But since OCD doesn't accept anything less than 100 percent certainty, a concept that exists only in terrible romance movies, you will probably not be convinced by this explanation. Slowly and progressively taking the risk of practicing nonavoidance and resisting compulsions is the best way to get there, and deliberate exposures can help.

Confronting Your Fears with Exposure

One of my harm OCD clients was an avid runner with a brilliant imagination. She reported that her symptoms made it so she was no longer able to enjoy her long morning runs without experiencing vivid images of pushing passersby into oncoming traffic or knocking over frail elderly neighbors. Her OCD had hijacked her creativity and interrupted one of her favorite activities. She had attempted everything to clear her mind of these thoughts. She listened to uplifting podcasts, practiced mantras to remind herself of her true character, and avoided running by the senior living community close to her house. Not surprisingly, the thoughts multiplied.

I suggested doing an about-face to practice exposure. As she was a huge podcast aficionado, her exposure would be to choose from the pantheon of true-crime podcasts and commit to listening to one every time she ran.

"But that will make it impossible not to think about hurting people while I'm running!" she protested.

"Well, you're already thinking about that now, aren't you?" I countered.

"But what if it makes me even more likely to hurt people? What if I like the podcast too much?"

"Are you willing to take that—"

"Ugh, yes," she interrupted. "I'm willing to take that risk."

There's no shortage of media with violent themes. If you're a movie buff, there are entire genres and subgenres to explore with violent content. There are television shows predicated on unsolved crimes and miniseries and documentaries about survivors of rape, assault, and torture. If you love music, you can create a playlist of songs that contain triggering words or that tell stories from people who have experienced violence. The goal is not to engage with violent content just for the sake of it, but to reclaim from your OCD a type of media that you enjoy. And again, remember the function here: my client was avoiding anything that would remind her of violence, so I asked her to lean into it. If she were ruminating excessively rather than avoiding triggers, we would have taken another approach.

You Can Do It!

Whew! It seems important to stop here to acknowledge just how difficult the work on these themes is. Many of us from childhood onward are inundated with messages about morality and how to be a decent or upstanding person in relation to others. *Be a good boy or girl. Don't lust after others. Show the best version of yourself to others. Follow the Ten Commandments. Don't stray outside the lines.* Harm OCD and ROCD can make you feel like you're challenging these teachings. SO-OCD and gender-related OCD can too if you were raised in a culture with overt rules about sexuality and gender. I know that it seems like a gargantuan task to cast away what OCD has convinced you is a safety net for your own morality. My clients often tell me that it's like I'm walking them to the edge of a cliff and encouraging them to jump even though they can't see the safe landing through the fog of OCD's clouds. I'm here to validate that if you're feeling overwhelmed, it's understandable and it means that you're probably hitting OCD where it hurts.

The themes in this chapter can particularly impact relationships. They are also all OC-normal, and you can approach these symptoms with the same tools that you would use with any other theme. If you didn't see yourself or your own symptoms in this chapter, that's okay too. In the following chapters, you will learn how to address all different kinds of OCD across different relationship types, starting with friendships.

CHAPTER 4

The Family You Choose
Friendship and OCD

Friends occupy a unique place in our social worlds. They make up the network that we choose to affiliate with, not the one we were born into or the ones (immediate family or work colleagues) to whom we feel obligated. Our choice in the matter makes these connections even more special. Although we don't have any legal ties to friends, we create our own language to legitimize and sanctify our bonds. As children, we may name our friend groups (shout out to the Totally Cool Girls Club of 1990), develop secret handshakes, or devise code words for covert communication. We may bestow upon others the superlative of Best Friend or Oldest Friend or Friend Who's Never Going to Talk About What Happened That One Night. Friends make life easier, more enjoyable, more meaningful, and just generally better. Sounds like a perfect thing for OCD to disrupt, right? Well, even though it might try, you can take steps to find, build, and deepen fulfilling friendships while living with OCD.

Not much has been written about the impact of OCD on friendships. One study of the friendship networks of adults with OCD found no relationship between having OCD and friendship quality or closeness (Himle et al. 2017). That is, those with OCD were no more likely than those without it to have difficulties with friends, even though OCD was associated with negative interactions in family relationships. It's been suggested that because friendships are relationships of choice, people may deliberately find friends who are more accepting of their symptoms. Other studies focusing on children, however, have found that youth with OCD have more difficulties with peers compared with kids without mental health concerns; they may have fewer friends, more trouble making friends, more bullying experiences, and greater worries about being criticized by peers (Borda et al. 2013). As if having OCD weren't hard enough on its own!

Many adults living with OCD will tell you that managing symptoms can make friendships harder. You may feel self-conscious about how your symptoms are perceived by others. You may feel reluctant to get close to others who could unwittingly provoke your symptoms. You may fear that your most embarrassing symptoms will be revealed. You may expect rejection, abandonment, or ridicule from potential friends if you talk to them about your symptoms. Or, almost as bad, you may expect that your friend will glibly chirp, "Oh yeah, I'm pretty OCD too!" leaving you in the unenviable position of either becoming a reluctant OCD educator or laughing it off. But friends are worth taking these risks.

Why Friends Matter So Much

Although friendship within the context of OCD hasn't been well studied, we do have evidence of how friendship enhances people's general well-being. Friends can offer both practical and emotional support, inspire joy and pleasure, provide companionship, and help us through difficult times. Friendship may offer protection against certain health outcomes, as people with satisfying and mutual friendships report lower levels of cardiovascular ailments, and they live longer than those who lack these relationships (Kent de Grey and Uchino 2020). When it comes to mental health, people with positive friendships have lower rates of depression and suicidal thoughts (Werner-Seidler et al. 2017). Interestingly, the quality of friendships is generally more important than the frequency of contact or number of friends, so even having one good friend can make a difference.

While we don't know exactly how friendship and depression influence each other—whether depressed people lack the energy to form emotional relationships or whether having friendships helps to prevent depression—this research finding does show that cultivating friendships is strongly associated with positive outcomes. And it matters what those friendships are like emotionally too. For example, another study found that having frequent negative interactions with friends was associated with higher rates of anxiety and depression symptoms (Bertera 2005). So, the take-home is to have high-quality, mutual friendships even if only a few.

Simon's Story

Simon's OCD symptoms started after he injured his shoulder playing pickup basketball in college. He became fixated on the injury and preoccupied with the idea that his body might have sustained permanent damage. Simon engaged in frequent body checking (such as rotating his right arm to examine range of motion) and developed a strict strength training routine in the hope of preventing injury elsewhere. Simon also focused on eating only "clean" foods and taking supplements that promised faster healing. As he concentrated on these aspects of his OCD, he devoted less time to maintaining connections with others. He stopped playing basketball with his friends and ignored their invitations. He told himself that he would be back in contact with them as soon as his shoulder healed, but weeks stretched into months without communication.

His roommate Lyle encouraged him to hang out with their mutual friends, but Simon refused, worried that the smokiness of the bars they frequented and the greasy food from their favorite pizza joints would harm him. At the end of the semester, a group of his friends planned a rafting trip to Colorado together; it would be a meaningful way to say good-bye to those who were graduating and moving out of the area, including Lyle. Fearing a reinjury of his shoulder, which he still wasn't sure had healed right, Simon opted to stay home. After his friends left, Simon looked for a new apartment and job on his own, and, at the urgent prompting of his parents, entered therapy. He was overcome by feelings of isolation and recognized that he needed some major changes in his life.

Simon and Lyle were close. He had talked with Lyle, for example, about his feelings when Simon's girlfriend ended their relationship unexpectedly, and Simon had supported Lyle through his parents' divorce. Although they had a sense of mutual trust, Simon had refrained from telling Lyle about his symptoms because he was worried that Lyle wouldn't know how to react. *What if I tell him I don't want to eat junk anymore, and he thinks that I'm being vain or that I'm getting an eating disorder? he wondered.* This fear stemmed in part from Simon's hunch that his own behavior probably was a little bit irrational. But in the way that OC-normal brains tend to work, Simon still felt compelled to follow his new eating and exercise rules, just in case. Lyle, in turn, saw Simon's withdrawal as a signal that he was no longer interested in their friendship. The Colorado trip felt like the last straw to him, and he stopped trying after that.

What happened between Lyle and Simon is common in friendships affected by OCD, especially after an onset or increase in symptoms. Emotional concerns like shame and embarrassment can begin to weave narratives about your desirability or fitness as a friend. *They'll never understand,* you tell yourself, cutting off the relationship to speed up what feels inevitable. In this way, your fear that the friendship will end becomes a self-fulfilling prophecy.

Emotional or physical contamination concerns can limit friendships as well, such as when a friend engages in behavior that your OCD deems risky, unethical, or gross. Or when OCD outright decides that your friend is risky, gross, or otherwise contaminated. Harm OCD symptoms can make you feel like you're at risk to hurt others physically or emotionally, and so you "protect" your friends by withdrawing. And sexually intrusive thoughts can take a platonic relationship and cast it into murky territory quickly. Follow that with an urge to compulsively confess these thoughts, and you may have a confused friend and a strained friendship.

The truth is that OCD symptoms are tricky enough to deal with on your own, and putting friends in the mix can increase the likelihood of symptoms getting provoked. So, it's understandable to want to withdraw a bit. However, that's letting OCD interfere with your social life. To commit to the difficult task of keeping friends, an excellent place to start is with identifying what truly matters to you.

Identifying What Matters to You

One feature of acceptance and commitment therapy involves helping you clarify your *values*, which are the principles that guide how you want to live your life. Identifying your values creates a sense of purpose and increases motivation you may need to tackle the tough work of changing your behavior. Values are different from goals, which are finite and can be checked off a list. Values are enduring concepts that can guide you throughout your life and continually infuse your actions with meaning.

I always tell people that my years in graduate school were some of the most fulfilling I've experienced, because studying clinical psychology was an ideal fit for many of my values, including curiosity, connection, imagination, and self-development. It was an intellectual playground, and I felt for the first time that I had found "my people" in my classmates. By delighting in the ways that grad school allowed me to express these values, I found that there was less emphasis on the end goal of attaining a few extra letters after my name. The journey might have been long and challenging, but I truly felt like it was a privilege to be on it—and that feeling carried me through, because I knew the work I was doing was meaningful to me. Doing treatment for OCD is a similarly difficult journey, and it helps to remind yourself of how the work you're doing will reconnect you with what you value most.

Creating new social connections when you have OCD can also feel like a lofty goal, something that might be too hard to do. In some ways it may feel easier not to even try to get close to others. OCD is great at emphasizing what you might lose by taking a risk, so to counteract this tendency, it's important to consider the flipside of what you will gain. Examining your values can provide a glimpse into these gains by helping you see how you might live a meaningful life alongside friends. The next exercise will help you explore your values.

What You May Gain: *Examining Your Values*

Read the following series of scenarios and respond to the questions underneath each one. These questions are designed to help you evaluate what matters most to you, not just in friendships but in life more broadly. Write down your answers on a separate piece of paper or in your journal.

1. Imagine you're walking in the woods at dusk and come upon a mysterious artifact, a softly glowing metal box with a dial on it pointing to the numbers 5, 10, and 25. When you touch the box, it projects a movie into the darkness with scenes from your life, five, ten, or twenty-five years in the future. With this box, you're able to observe yourself over the course of a day and view everything you do, everyone you interact with, and everywhere you go. What would you most like to see in your future? How would you like to be spending your time and with whom? Allow yourself to dream a bit as you envision your ideal life at each time interval.

2. Next to the box, you find an oddly shaped hat with the words "Brain Jumper 3000" written on the outside. When you place it on your head, you gain the ability to enter the minds of others and observe

their thoughts. Even better, you get to listen to their thoughts specifically about you. When you jump into the mind of your best friend, what do you hope to find that they think about you? How about when you jump into a family member's mind? What would you hope to hear from a romantic partner's mind? These questions should reflect your ideal answers as a friend, family member, or partner. If you don't have someone in that role right now, it's okay to create one and think about what you would love to hear them say!

3. Finally, you come upon a deep, still pond with a holographic shimmer on its surface. It looks inviting, so you kneel and dip your hand in. Suddenly, your loudest obsessive thoughts become whispers and your urges to engage in compulsions all but evaporate. A countdown appears on the surface of the water ticking down seven days, and you realize that you have the next week to live symptom free. What do you most want to do in the next 168 hours while your symptoms are at bay? Whom do you want to see? What do you want to accomplish without the influence of OCD?

Now that you've answered these questions, look back at your responses to pick out the kinds of qualities that arise as common themes. Create a list of these values in your journal, choosing from the list below and writing down other values that matter to you even if they're not listed here. You may note that in each of your responses, the theme of hard work comes up; in that case, perhaps "industry" is one of your values. You may see that you want to be engaged in activities and develop connections that allow you to help others, in which case "compassion" might be a value of yours. As you peruse this list, include any values that appeal to you even if they didn't come up naturally in the story. Remember that there are no right or wrong answers! Save your list of values, as it will come up in future exercises.

Adaptability	Honesty	Power
Adventure	Gratitude	Safety
Beauty	Growth	Security
Bravery	Harmony	Self-development
Compassion	Humility	Sensuality
Connectedness	Humor	Service
Creativity	Imagination	Spirituality
Curiosity	Independence	Spontaneity
Dependability	Industry	Tolerance
Diligence	Justice	Tradition
Faith	Kindness	Truth
Fitness	Liberty	Wisdom
Fun	Love	Work ethic

Awesome! You've identified your values.

As you review your list of words, pay special attention to the values that came up with the part of question 2 related to what you would want your best friend to think about you. We will use these later in the chapter to help you see how to live by these values in your friendships, even as OCD tries to thwart you.

Making Friends When You Have OCD

Finding friends as an adult can be brutal. Unlike the environments we're in when young—schools, extracurriculars—adulthood doesn't always afford us a built-in pool of potential mates. As a result, finding companions with whom you share common interests can be difficult (anyone want to start the Totally Cool *Adults* Club?). As adults, we are also more likely to move from one community, city, or town to another, and some friendships aren't suited to connecting over long distances.

You may have to get a little creative to find your crew, but thankfully there are ways to reduce your isolation and increase connectedness with others. Here are some places where you can put yourself out there as a grown-up, even if OCD protests:

- Working environment

- Faith-based community

- In the neighborhood

- Hobbies and clubs

- Sports

- Volunteer work

- OCD support groups

To get going on this, you can use the "Places to Make Friends When You Have OCD" worksheet, which is available at http://www.newharbin ger.com/50584.

What about if you're interested in some of these opportunities for making friends, but OCD has something to say about it? Maybe you'd love to go to synagogue, but your scrupulosity symptoms shoot through the roof the moment you enter the sanctuary. Perhaps you've been having hilarious conversations with your next-door neighbor, but you're worried about them contaminating your home if they stop over. If OCD is getting in the way, let's see if we can refute some of the thoughts your OCD might be sending you.

"It's too big a step." OCD tends to think about things in black-and-white terms. *Either I join a support group and spill everything about my OCD to strangers or I don't.* But wait—might there be an intermediate step to get there? Perhaps you can connect with people online before going to an in-person group if doing that feels more comfortable. Perhaps you can check with the group leader about easing into sharing information with others over time rather than right away. If it feels like diving into the deep end, step back and ask yourself if there's a way to dip a toe in first. It still may be uncomfortable, but most worthwhile things are.

"I'll be rejected or ridiculed." OCD loves for you to feel like you have control, and social situations can easily shatter that illusion. Interacting with another person means that they bring their own beliefs, interpretations, feelings, and behaviors into the equation. And in the range of possible interaction outcomes, if A represents the best possible result and Z the worst, OCD likes to focus on the XYZ options. I'm not asking you to dismiss the possibility of rejection; to be human and open to relationships with others, we all must accept this possibility. I'm asking you to allow yourself to consider the possibility that things could go well. Squint your eyes and look a little further up the alphabet. Check in with your values and what you might gain, and then see if you can take that chance.

"I can't do it." One of the biggest lies that OCD tells you is that you can't do things that are difficult. The truth is that it's not a matter of ability; it's a matter of your willingness to try. You likely have the necessary skills but haven't used them for a while because OCD has had the reins. This truth may seem harsh, and you may feel a bloom of anger at being called "unwilling." But all too often we wait around until things feel right before acting, which leads to…well…a lot of waiting. You may not *want* to take the risk of meeting new people, but that doesn't mean you *can't*. Willingness is the opposite of this; it's embracing the uncertainty and fear that come with vulnerable and scary actions. Think about something that used to scare you as a child and how you overcame it. Chances are you overcame your fear because of repeated exposure to it, whether or not you felt ready. The good news as an adult is that you get to choose when you're ready. And why not now?

"It will trigger my symptoms more." This one's often true, depending on what kinds of situations and personal characteristics your OCD hooks onto. If so, it's up to you to decide if the risk of facing your fears outweighs the benefit of starting and deepening social connections. Revisiting your values may be helpful here too. And if you're unsure if the interaction will trigger your symptoms, then ask if you might be XYZing yourself out of a possible connection.

"I don't deserve to be close to others." Self-punishment is one of the most heartbreaking reasons why people with OCD neglect making friends. As humans, we are wired for connection, and you're worthy of having gratifying friendships just as much as anyone else. As someone living with OCD and confronting painful symptoms, it may be particularly important for you to have a support system. Having others in your life who will love and accept you can help you see yourself in a softer and more compassionate light. Revisit the self-compassion exercise in chapter 1 to allow yourself to open to the care you deserve.

Keeping Friends When You Have OCD

Like all relationships, friendships take work to maintain. They thrive when both parties feel that they're contributing to and getting something out of the union. You may find that your OCD topples the economy of the friendship over to one side, creating strain and resentment. This can occur when well-meaning friends engage in symptom accommodation to reduce your distress but quickly find out that no amount of "helping" makes you feel better for long. They've told you repeatedly that they've never gotten sick at the new Thai place downtown, but you keep asking for reassurance or canceling plans to meet there. Friends may wonder why your communication is inconsistent, or if they said something wrong or offended you. They may wonder why you avoid doing certain activities, or why when you used to love watching horror movies together, suddenly they're off-limits. Having an honest conversation with friends about your symptoms can let them know that it's nothing personal and can allow them to be part of your support team.

Balancing Risk and Reward in Disclosure

Sharing with someone else that you have OCD is a big step in any relationship. It can allow others to fully see you in your vulnerability and can alleviate some of the burden of shouldering your symptoms. Friends who understand your OCD are less likely to misinterpret repetitive questions as nagging, or lateness as a personal affront. They can contextualize your behavior through the lens of the invisible beast you're wrestling with. They can also offer support when things are overwhelming and celebrate your treatment successes with you. However, disclosure also comes with risk. We need look no further than how OCD has been depicted in popular media to see that simply disclosing your OCD status is unlikely to create understanding on its own; indeed, it can sometimes lead to stigma. As nice as it would be to have an OCD Fairy visit your friends and infuse them with instant wisdom and compassion, the work of educating others will likely come down to you. And because explaining the ins and out of such a complex phenomenon takes time and energy (try writing a book about it!), it's worthwhile to consider a few things when making this decision.

If you have a friend you're contemplating telling about your OCD, first consider the emotional tone of your friendship as a whole. Even though you haven't disclosed your OCD, you have likely had some experience talking about other difficult things. When you confided in your friend, how did they respond? Were they able to listen and validate that this must have been hard for you? Did they offer advice or just listen well? Did they minimize your experience or criticize your response? A kind and empathic response may indicate that your friend is likely to respond similarly to your disclosure about OCD. If your friend tends to be more of a problem solver who likes to give advice, you can preface your disclosure by mentioning that you don't want advice so much as someone to listen.

It's also important to think about your motivations in sharing. Sometimes OCD can sneakily make disclosure a moral issue, telling you that if you don't tell others about your OCD, you're basically lying to them. This leap in logic, brought to you by our old friend moral scrupulosity, can provide temporary relief followed by confusion for both you and your friend. That is, maybe you tell someone whom you're not actually that close to about your OCD symptoms in a way that they find off-putting rather than helpful. Or you might worry that you didn't explain it correctly, leading you to clarify over and over. Remember that where there's urgency, OCD may not be far behind. OCD can also lead to over-explaining in an effort to make sure that your friend understands every last detail of your experience. Slow down and take your time, as they'll likely need some time to digest things.

What you tell your friends and how much you tell them is entirely up to you, however. You may want to start with talking about symptoms that are easier to explain before getting into some of the more complex ones. You can use behavioral examples that they might have seen, such as saying, "Hey, so you know how I always look in my rearview mirror a lot?" before diving into some of the fears that underlie the behaviors. You can share videos, articles, or other materials that you think might be helpful. And although it might be tempting to ask them to help you with rituals or other forms of accommodation, try instead to let them know how they can be better collaborators in your journey toward wellness. That might mean coming up with an arrangement to gradually try out things together that your OCD likes you to avoid, or it might mean talking about appropriate ways for them to rebuff reassurance seeking.

It's possible that some people will react in hurtful ways when you tell them about your OCD. These reactions can vary from the simply misinformed ("I didn't think you could be messy and have OCD!") to the profoundly insensitive ("You just need to try harder"). Others may react with bewilderment or may withdraw due to their own struggles. In any one of these cases, it's important that you treat yourself with care and compassion. If someone is ultimately unable to handle discussing your OCD, it means that they lack the wherewithal to do so—and not that you have failed. Also remember that your choice to disclose doesn't define the relationship. Not everyone needs to know about your OCD, and you might not feel that every friendship needs this kind of intimate disclosure.

Creating Your Friendship Exposure Hierarchy

Creating an exposure hierarchy can provide you with a blueprint for easing into doing things with friends that are currently difficult because of OCD. For example, Simon cared about physical fitness, but he had stopped almost all exercise by the time he started therapy for his OCD. Because most of his friends enjoyed spending time together exercising or playing sports, he was missing out on spending time with them *and* neglecting to engage in this value. When he created an exposure hierarchy in this example, he listed "fitness" as a value in the first column and then three exposures (or activities) in the next column based on this value. He also listed a fourth exposure for "humor." He then rated each of his exposures on a scale of 1 to 10 to indicate his willingness to try them out.

Value	Friendship Exposure	Willingness
Fitness	Going for a hike with Andre	8
Fitness	Shooting some hoops with Pete	5
Fitness	Playing a full game of basketball	2
Humor	Going to trivia night	6

Simon used this hierarchy as a guide for trying out new behaviors, starting with the ones he was most willing to do at first and gradually working his way up to the most difficult exposures.

Now it's your turn to fill out a "Friendship Exposure Hierarchy," which is available at http://www.newharbinger.com/50584. First review your list of values from the exercise you did earlier in this chapter, paying particular attention to your responses in question 2 about your best friend. From this list, choose three to five values that describe how you want to behave as a friend. Write these values at the top of the worksheet. In the first column, list those values that you want to express but currently avoid. Then in the second column, write down some activities that you'd like to be able to do with friends to express these values; list these activities from least to most difficult to do.

If you're having a hard time generating any examples for exposures, you can do these steps in reverse order. That is, think of something that you avoid doing with friends and then see if you can tie it back in to one of your values. For example, Simon knew that he'd stopped going to trivia nights with his friends because they were held at a restaurant that he felt was unhealthy. So he wrote "Going to trivia night" on his exposure list and then asked himself what value this activity most represented. Given that his trivia buddies were some of the funniest people he knew, he chose "humor" as his value.

After you write down your exposures, rate each one on a scale of 1 to 10 to indicate how willing you are to try it, where 1 indicates that you're definitely unwilling to try this exposure now and 10 means that you're willing to jump in as soon as possible. Then use this hierarchy as a guide for trying out new behaviors, starting with the ones you're most willing to do and gradually working your way up to the most challenging ones.

Being Your Own Best Friend

When you have OCD, pursuing and maintaining friendships can feel tricky or intimidating. You may have doubts about your ability to get close to people or even feel like you don't deserve friendship. You may find yourself withdrawing in an attempt to avoid potentially awkward interactions. But friendship, like anything else that's important, is worth the risk. I hope that this chapter has given you some ideas about how to challenge your thoughts and change your behaviors to move toward meaningful connections. If this is tough, then you can start by being your own best friend: showering yourself with the support and pep talks that you need to branch out. You can also extend that role to being your own wing-person, because in the next chapter, we will be talking about dating and love.

CHAPTER 5

Putting Yourself Out There
Dating, Romance, and OCD

You deserve to find love. Yes, you! You deserve love even with the frightening thoughts that course through your mind. You deserve love even if you're struggling to fend off rituals, stuck in doubt, and feeling not quite ready. In fact, OCD in all its fussiness may *never* allow you to feel ready.

There's a story that ACT therapists use to illustrate this, called "Waiting for the Wrong Train" (Stoddard and Afari 2014). In this story, you're at a train station waiting to go to an exciting destination; for the purposes of this chapter, we'll call it Smittentown. Plenty of trains are headed to Smittentown; in fact, they come and go frequently. The problem is that the train cars are crowded and uncomfortable with threadbare seats and broken air conditioning. What's more, you don't feel entirely ready to board the train, especially not a train in this condition. So, you decide to wait until a nicer train comes along, one with room for you to stretch out, relax, and enjoy the journey. As you wait, you see fellow passengers hopping on and departing for Smittentown. You stand alone for hours and then days, waiting for the perfect train to arrive. And you think things like, *Once my OCD is better, I'll start looking. Once I feel more confident, I'll go on a date.* All the while, you get no closer to your destination. It's time to ask yourself if you're willing to follow your heart and board that ramshackle train, an apt metaphor for twenty-first-century dating if ever there was one!

There's so much to gain from romantic relationships. These relationships combine the companionship of friendship with physical closeness, increased intimacy, and the possibility of shared finances, family building, and visions of a future together. And then there are the intangibles: you meet someone and find that their jawline scrambles your ability to form coherent sentences. Their smile feels like it was built just for you. A special network of nicknames, inside jokes, and traditions blooms up around you. While not every romantic relationship has all these components, each relationship constitutes an intricate little world created by two people who've chosen one another. People with romantic connections are generally happier, healthier, and more likely to feel supported in their mental health journeys. This goes for childless couples, those in the LGBTQIA+ elsewhere community, people in consensually nonmonogamous relationships, asexual partners—everyone across the relational spectrum. Everyone deserves and benefits from love, including you.

In this chapter, we'll cover how best to cultivate and nurture your romantic relationships while OCD tries its best to keep you alone at the train station. I'll provide information on overcoming roadblocks to dating, exploring your attachment style, disclosing your OCD symptoms to partners, strengthening your bonds, and applying evidence-based treatment methods to thrive with your partner.

Loving Others When It's Hard to Love Yourself

You may believe the cliché that you need to love yourself before you can love someone else. But believing this isn't very helpful, especially to the OC-normal brain. It's hard to feel love for yourself when you have symptoms that feel bizarre, illogical, or shameful. And how can you know if you love yourself without a shadow of a doubt? Is there a test for it? If so, will your perfectionistic brain allow you to pass it?

The good news is that you don't have to ace any self-love tests before finding romantic connections. In fact, opening yourself up to others is in itself an act of self-love. Pursuing romance is not asserting that you're perfect but rather that you're worthy of affection, flaws and all. Think about the self-compassion exercise at the end of chapter 1. In this exercise, you identified some of the stories that your OCD tells you about who you can be in relationships and what you can offer to others. Instead of putting each of these thoughts on trial and gathering evidence to refute them, you simply allowed these thoughts to be there and chose to see them as a part of the human experience of suffering. You held them softly in your mind as you practiced treating yourself with kindness. Holding your thoughts, even the messy, self-critical ones, in kindness is the first step toward rewriting the stories penned by OCD.

So take a moment to consider: what do you want when it comes to relationships? Do you want to date? Are you in a relationship already that you'd like to strengthen? Do you find that your OCD symptoms are sometimes interfering in your relationship and want to know what to do about that? We'll explore all these topics in this chapter, but it can help to clarify what you're looking for before diving in.

Dating with OCD

Some of my clients seeking romantic connections are doing so for the first time and want practical guidance on how to approach dating. If that's you, congratulations on your willingness to take this step! As with finding friends, a good place to start when looking for partners is by clarifying where and how you like to spend your time. Meeting someone with shared interests will increase your chances of compatibility. This can mean looking in the places that you already know, like your gym, volunteer meetings, worship services, school, or work. Meeting people through shared social connections can be helpful too, as friends may have insight into how well you'll connect with others. And there are scores of ways to meet people online, using apps, sites, or forums.

If you try dating apps, your OCD may try to dictate exactly how you portray yourself online, so beware of its pull. Moral scrupulosity may demand that you be up-front about all your flaws so as to avoid "false advertising." Just right symptoms may have you writing and rewriting your profile or agonizing over which pictures to choose. But this can also be a wonderful opportunity to practice getting it done without becoming swept up in a wave of compulsive perfecting. If you're finding that your brain wants perfection, be creative! Set a timer for how long you'll spend on these apps. Make a spelling error on purpose. Let a friend choose your pictures (one friend, no second opinions, without reassurance!) for you. These exposures are unlikely to significantly change your outcome—despite what OCD may tell you, few people really notice a spelling error on a dating profile, and the kind of person who makes wild judgments based on the pictures they see probably isn't someone you'd want to date anyway—but they do give you an opportunity to take that risk and fight your OCD.

It's also true that because dating is about seeking mutual compatibility, you can expect to experience rejection along the way. This is a hard pill to swallow for perfectionists and those who tie their self-worth to others' perceptions. It can also be a field day for ROCD symptoms and lead to grueling mental postmortems after "failed" interactions: *What did I say? How could I have acted differently? If only I'd done this instead.* Rather than tormenting yourself with these questions, I'd encourage you to see rejections as necessary speed bumps on the road toward finding connection and be willing to experience them in service of the value of romantic connection. When OCD suggests that your shortcomings are the only reason for the rejection, consider that everyone brings their own unique needs, preferences, and attachment styles to this process. Your would-be partner may be looking for someone very different from you, and you deserve someone who's going to love you for who you are. If you're a round peg meeting square holes, the problem isn't in your roundness. It's that you haven't found someone whose edges are soft enough yet.

You too will likely let some people down. While it can be gut-wrenching to let someone know that you're uninterested, rejecting someone doesn't make you a bad person any more than being rejected does. Treating one another with respect and honesty ensures that you can pull things out of romantic territory in the kindest way possible. And while you can't ensure how your words will be received—see, for example, the entire genre of breakup music—you can feel better knowing that you've freed yourself and the other person to find something more fulfilling.

I imagine that if you have ROCD, your heart rate might be elevated reading this chapter. How do you know when to bring up relationship concerns, and how do you know that they're real enough to warrant a discussion? Even if there were a clear-cut answer to this question, your OCD wouldn't accept it. So, my challenge to you is to continue reading without the requirement that you figure it out.

A Few Words About Attachment

Does your response to potential romantic partners sometimes remind you of how you interacted with your parents or caretakers when you were a child? According to attachment theory, our understanding about the world indeed starts with our early experiences as a baby. Many of us found that if we were hungry or uncomfortable, someone would predictably respond to our needs and soothe us, and in this way, we developed a secure attachment style (as mentioned in chapter 1). We came to believe that we deserved caretaking and could readily ask for soothing, which can carry over to adult relationships too.

Others of us learned that we couldn't always rely on our caregivers to respond in helpful ways, and as a result we developed anxiety about relationships and doubted our ability to trust others. We may have begun worrying about our worthiness to receive love, clung to any positive attention, or become ultraindependent to avoid being let down by others. These patterns, broadly called *insecure attachment,* may have persisted throughout our childhoods and even into adulthood, popping up in romantic relationships.

Attachment Anxiety and Avoidance

When talking about attachment, it's helpful to consider two concepts: anxiety and avoidance. *Attachment anxiety* shows up as concerns about the availability of your partner and fears of abandonment. *Attachment avoidance* looks like a fear of closeness and protectiveness over your independence. These two concepts exist on a continuum, and everyone experiences some degree of each. If you're low in both anxiety and avoidance in a relationship, you're securely attached. If you're high on anxiety but low on avoidance, you may have a form of insecure attachment that leads you to engage in excessive reassurance seeking and to worry frequently about abandonment. If you're low in anxiety and high in avoidance, you may have a form of insecure attachment that leads you to appear withdrawn from others and to always be on the lookout for the closest metaphorical exit in your relationships. If you're high in both anxiety and avoidance, you may swing between strong emotions in your relationship and have a hard time finding your footing. This can look like alternately seeking contact with your partner and pushing them away.

None of these attachment styles is a death sentence for relationships, nor does your attachment style in childhood always manifest in your adult relationships. That is, although early experiences are important, we aren't simply passive products of our childhood interactions. We have opportunities to refine and revise our attachment over time with each new relationship we embrace. Knowing your tendency toward one or another attachment style, however, can help you understand why your relationship anxiety or avoidance manifests how it does.

Self Exploration: *Identifying Your Relationship Anxiety and Avoidance*

Look at the chart and write down the statements that resonate with you. This exercise is loosely based on the work of Simpson, Rholes, and Phillips (1996).

Anxious Attachment	Avoidant Attachment
I worry that my partners will leave me.	I worry that partners may stifle my independence.
I wonder if my partners really love me.	I don't like depending on partners.
I want more closeness than my partners do.	Getting close to partners is hard.
I feel insecure about my partners' care for me.	I don't like it when partners need me.
I can come off as clingy with my partners.	Trusting partners is hard for me.

The more statements you identified in the first column, the more likely you may tend toward attachment anxiety; the more statements you identified in the second column, the more likely you tend toward attachment avoidance.

Enter OCD stage left with a pocketful of unknowable questions and a flourish of dramatic music. Not surprisingly, people with more features of OCD tend to score higher on measures of both attachment anxiety and avoidance (Van Leeuwen et al. 2020). Feeling ashamed about your symptoms or worrying about the impact of compulsions on your relationship can make you feel like you can detect "evidence" that your partner will never accept you, leading to increased attachment anxiety. Perfectionism and rigid standards can make you doubt that any partner will live up to your ideals, leading to attachment avoidance.

To begin thinking about how your OCD amps up your attachment anxiety or avoidance, you can ask yourself these questions:

1. How does OCD impact my beliefs about my lovability?

2. How does OCD make me feel less able to connect with others?

3. How does OCD change my notions of dependence or independence?

4. How does OCD place idealistic standards on what a relationship should look like?

5. How does OCD create rules about dating or relationships?

If answering these questions is challenging or makes you feel vulnerable, you're not alone! But doing so can help to unpack some of the baggage that OCD can heap on your relationship worries. For example, one of my clients with harm OCD discussed how he felt his avoidant attachment style was exacerbated by his OCD. "It's already hard for me to get close to people without feeling smothered," he told me. "And now my OCD is telling me that I'm dangerous too! So, it's like I have even more reasons to run away from people when we start getting close."

In response to this revelation, the client and I talked about the importance of living by his values, and how some of his behaviors, like withdrawing and meticulously planning each date to avoid harm, were preventing him from fulfilling his values of adventure, connection, and humor.

These questions can also spark a conversation with your partner (or partners) about how they see OCD entering the relationship. Knowing your attachment style can also inform your ability to refrain from compulsions. Having a high level of attachment anxiety, for example, can create a sense of urgency to verify the status of the relationship, leading to checking. Treating yourself with compassion may look like telling yourself this: *Wow, this is really hard because I tend to have higher attachment anxiety. However, I can practice sitting with these feelings without trying to resolve them right away.*

There are other things you can do to strengthen a romantic relationship despite what your instincts or your OCD might tell you. Next we'll explore some ways to nurture the romantic connections you build.

Nurturing Your Romantic Connections

Drs. John and Julie Gottman have studied the components of healthy romantic relationships for over forty years. Collectively, they have published hundreds of academic articles and books, including research with newlyweds that predicted with over 90 percent accuracy which couples would divorce over time. If this conjures up images of becloaked mystics gazing into a crystal ball, the reality is even cooler: we have data on what works for couples to maintain happy and long-lasting relationships. These principles form what the Gottmans call the "Sound Relationship House" theory (Gottman and Gottman 2017) and include things like getting to know your partner's inner world, sharing admiration for one another, being responsive to each other, assuming the best about your partner, supporting their growth, and managing conflict well. With or without OCD, all relationships can benefit from these various components.

Let's explore some aspects of the Gottmans' theory, beginning with the foundation of romantic intimacy: getting to know one another's inner worlds. Like it or not, OCD is a core part of your world, so it's worth thinking about how you might disclose your symptoms to your partner.

How to Tell Your Partners About OCD

Oh no, you might think. *I'm not sure that my partner wants to see the kinds of things that are playing out in my head!* But telling your partners about OCD doesn't mean unleashing a stream of consciousness of every thought, impulse, or urge you experience. It means sharing some of the things that make you unique. What you reveal about yourself doesn't have to be emotionally loaded or even particularly deep at first; it can be sharing your favorite movies, talking about how you spend your free time, and learning about each other's siblings. Over time, as intimacy deepens, sharing more vulnerable parts of your inner world becomes valuable too. After all, if a person is going to be part of your life, it's pretty important that they're part of your *whole life,* or at least the biggest parts. And if you're reading a book about OCD right now, chances are that OCD's a big enough part to consider sharing.

Questions about when to disclose are among the most common that I'm typically asked. Understandably, people want to know how to effectively reveal private and sometimes painful information in a way that will bring them closer to loved ones. And as with almost any other important thing in life, there's no guarantee that it will go the way that you planned. In this way, disclosure is a form of exposure: you must be willing to accept the risk that your partner may not react in a supportive way.

If you're willing to take this risk, start by examining your motivation. There are so many reasons to share, some of which are likely to help you nurture intimacy and some of which are more likely to nurture OCD symptoms. You may want to ask yourself if you're disclosing out of a sense of obligation (*They should know the mess they're getting into* or *If I don't tell them, I'm lying*) or as an apology for having OCD (*I'm so sorry that I'm messed up, and I get it if you want to leave*). If so, your disclosure may be rooted in shame, embarrassment, or anxiety rather than a genuine desire to be open about yourself to strengthen your connection. Talking about it may provide short-term relief for the discomfort that OCD can cause, but the disclosure won't serve you well in the long term if this is your reason for talking about OCD; ultimately, it can be a self-centered motive in that you end up putting your anxiety about your symptoms first rather than the realities or health of your relationship.

MOVING TOWARD WHAT'S IMPORTANT

Another way to approach disclosure is to see if it's what ACT therapists call a *toward* move or an *away* move. Toward moves bring us closer to things that are important to us, while away moves serve to reduce anxiety, discomfort, or other unwanted emotions. A toward move would be disclosing your OCD so that your partner understands your behavior better and can support you, while an away move would serve to provide quick and temporary relief from discomfort. What fears do you notice getting in the way of disclosure? Do you have any evidence that these fears would play out based on past behavior? Notice if you find yourself ruminating on this last question, trying to get some elusive certainty. If fears are motivating your decisions, you might be engaging in an away move.

Remember that there's no reason that you have to tell anyone everything about your symptoms right away. Disclosure can be offered in small bits, allowing you to open up while retaining a sense of privacy about details you're reluctant to reveal. Maybe you want to reveal that you have mental health concerns without labeling the OCD itself. Or perhaps you want to talk about the symptoms that are most visible before going into the ones that your partner might not be aware of. Providing your loved one with resources about OCD may be helpful too. Books, blog posts, social media accounts, or websites can all enhance their understanding without putting the burden of education all on you.

Again, disclosure is an exposure because you can't control the outcome, and that means being willing to accept whatever comes next after you reveal your OCD. It doesn't mean liking how it feels or approving of your partner's response, but it does mean accepting reality as it is. For example, if I were to wake up on the day of running a marathon (a purely hypothetical event, I can assure you) and discover that the weather was blustery, I could accept the cold and the rain without liking it or trying to change it. Your relationship meteorology after a disclosure may feel cooler or warmer than expected; your partner might react with surprising calm and understanding, or they might find the disclosure difficult to process or accept. But trying to predict this accurately is like… well, like trying to predict the weather. It doesn't always go well. Nor does it often change what you end up having to do. The marathoner who wakes up on a windy, rainy day will probably run the marathon anyway, accepting what's there even if they don't entirely like it. But when the marathon is done, they'll know they completed it because it was something that mattered, just as you'll know that disclosure for the sake of greater intimacy is ultimately important, no matter the outcome.

PREPARING FOR DISCLOSURE

To prepare for disclosing to others, you'll need to think about what you want to say to your partners, either current or prospective, about your OCD and how you want to say it. I suggest writing down what's important for you to say and how you'd like to say it. Here's an example:

I have OCD. I wanted to tell you about it because I'd love to have your support when it's rearing up. I also wanted you to know so that when I'm struggling, you can have a context for my behavior and won't think that I'm withdrawing or getting stuck because of something you've done. I'm not ready to tell you about all my symptoms because some of them are a little tough to talk about. But I wanted to start the conversation.

Note that this example establishes some boundaries around what's up for discussion, which is an avenue you can definitely take. Disclosing your OCD is something foundational to the kinds of shared inner worlds that make for strong relationships. It's also something that can and should happen at a pace that's comfortable for you and your partner.

Strengthening Your Bonds

After building the foundation of shared inner worlds, the next building blocks of a positive relationship involve deepening a mutual sense of trust, support, and affection. As already discussed, the OC-normal brain can be sneaky about mixing up positive support and unhelpful symptom accommodation. That is, it might feel helpful for your partner to take care of the bills instead of you spending hours caught up in checking and rechecking. However, over time, this arrangement can both reduce your ability to address this compulsion and increase the conflict in your relationship. A better way for your partner to support you is by learning everything they can about OCD and helping you ride the waves of anxiety that come with doing fewer compulsions. This may mean that you practice tolerating uncertainty together and create a mutual culture of pushing yourselves outside of your comfort zones.

The Gottmans' research also shows that sharing admiration is a crucial part of a healthy relationship. You may want to take a moment right now to reflect on what you appreciate about your partner(s). (Or, if you're not currently in a relationship, you can think about a past partner or even think of someone you've had a crush on if you're new to dating!) It may be helpful to think back to when you first met them and the feelings that arose at that time. Maybe they demonstrated a kindness toward your symptoms or showed grit in persevering through difficult circumstances. Maybe they helped you unlock the very best version of yourself or displayed creativity that left you in awe. Now, consider this: how often do you express these thoughts to your partner? And how about when these thoughts arise on a day-to-day basis—do you stop to let your partner know how much you admire them? Even if you prefer to show your affection nonverbally, consider sporadically sharing these things aloud. By expressing specific areas of admiration, your partner can feel seen and appreciated.

Responding to your partner's attempts to receive support and comfort—or "bids" as the Gottmans call them—with attentiveness and care also strengthens your relationship. A bid can be something simple like smiling or sharing a funny story, or it can be something more complex like asking for help with solving a problem. Responsiveness to your partner is a simple way to show them that you respect them and that you're listening. Unfortunately, OCD can undermine this process by distracting you with looping thoughts or repetitive behaviors that drown out others' bids. And if a partner interrupts you in the middle of a lengthy compulsion, a bid may even turn into a fight. If this has been part of your relationships, there's no need to beat yourself up. However, you can communicate to your partner that while you want to be responsive, you sometimes struggle with dividing attention. This discussion can help the two of you get back on the same page to work through the OCD together and make sure that bids on both sides are met with the attention, affirmation, and validation they warrant.

Steering Clear of Blame

Another feature of successful relationships is that both parties assume the best about each other and are not quick to blame. This means that when your partner does something that bothers you, like failing to text when they've arrived safely for a work trip, you give them the benefit of the doubt. Maybe they got sidetracked talking to their boss or failed to properly charge their phone. Maybe they simply forgot. But failing to text does not necessarily mean that they no longer love you or take your requests seriously.

I see conflicts around blame come up in a few ways for couples affected by OCD. Sometimes people with OCD assume that their partners are deliberately harming them when their partners prevent them from completing a ritual "correctly" or when a partner's behavior triggers anxiety. On the other hand, sometimes partners chalk up everything to OCD and therefore show little sympathy for any expression of anxiety, or they abruptly remove all symptom accommodation without any discussion or mutual decision making. Assuming the best—that you can be honest with your partner about your symptoms and how they're affecting you and the relationship, and about how your partner's behavior may be affecting your symptoms in return—decreases criticism and defensiveness in the relationship. Assuming the best is a way to show your partner that you believe they're fundamentally kind. It also allows you to support one another in your growth toward individual or shared goals. And having the shared goal of minimizing OCD's impact can yield a beautiful collaboration.

Of course, every relationship has some level of conflict. In fact, you may have noticed that you and your partner have the same few fights over and over. This is actually common, and more than half of couples report experiencing repetitive, unresolved conflicts. (And, if you ask my husband, 99 percent of these are about *how you just won't put your dishes in the dishwasher when it's right there*.) With OCD, conflict can be complicated by symptoms. There may be increased criticism, hostility, and overinvolvement between partners or poor communication, all of which can negatively affect both individual and relationship functioning (Abramowitz et al. 2013).

Ultimately, it's how conflict is managed that differentiates strong couples from couples who push each other away. A little gentleness goes a long way. If you're angry with your partner and feel like you're about to blow up at them, it's helpful to catch this and to step back and soothe yourself before confronting them. This ensures that you'll be kinder in your approach and minimizes the likelihood of escalating the conflict. However, it's also important not to confuse self-soothing with doing a mental compulsion! If you take a moment to withdraw from your partner to complete a rumination, your brain is learning that your relationship with OCD is more important than the relationship in front of you.

Negotiation and flexibility are crucial in relationships as well. Entering a relationship means that you're willing to compromise your personal preferences to some degree to support your partner's aspirations. It also means that you'll consider your own needs alongside your partner's and work together to come to resolution whenever these might clash. The balance between assertiveness and compromise is going to look different for every relationship, but being neither passive nor aggressive about your desires can strike a sweet spot. Remember that OCD may have quite a few opinions about how things should go as well, but it doesn't need to have a permanent place at the table.

Jamal's Story

Jamal always had a soft spot for children and knew from an early age he wanted to be a father. As the oldest of ten cousins, he delighted in babysitting during family gatherings at his grandmother's house. In college, he volunteered at the local Boys & Girls Club, providing mentorship and support for neighborhood children. So, when after four years of marriage, Jamal and his husband, Jack, decided to adopt a baby, he was over the moon. He had little doubt that he would be a devoted and adoring father. His OCD, however, was less convinced. Early into the adoption process, Jamal began having intrusive thoughts about harming or sexually assaulting their future child.

Having gone through ERP, Jamal tried his best to mindfully notice the thoughts and refocus on the present, but it was grueling. He considered trying another round of therapy to deal with his latest symptoms, but the adoption was expensive, and it seemed wisest to devote money to that. On the other hand, he reasoned that if he was even slightly at risk of harming a child, he shouldn't be moving forward with the decision at all. Jamal began frequently seeking reassurance and avoided any potential contact with children. Additionally, to minimize his triggers, he delegated many of the adoption tasks to Jack.

Jack had been slower to warm up to the idea of expanding their family and was resentful that his husband was casting doubt on the long and expensive adoption process. He felt betrayed in that Jamal had so strongly championed the idea of having a baby and was now leaving all the work to him. He knew that providing reassurance was unhelpful for Jamal's OCD but felt exhausted by constantly deflecting questions. So he gave in, letting his husband know that Of course he wasn't a monster, and Of course he would love the baby. This, in turn, exacerbated Jamal's symptoms, as his OCD declared that he would be the exception to the rule that Jack was laying out and would follow through with his terrible thoughts. In couples therapy, both

*Jamal and Jack were tired and hopeless, stating that they were in
a constant state of tension. Jack felt like he had to tiptoe around
triggering topics, and Jamal felt like his OCD was driving a wedge
between them. "This was supposed to be the happiest time of my life,"
he said tearfully. "What happened?"*

*Family was a priority for Jamal, which is precisely why OCD
decided to infiltrate this special time in his life. To make matters
more complicated, Jamal tended toward an anxious attachment style,
while Jack was more avoidant. When there was conflict, Jamal
sought validation that Jack still loved him. Jack, on the other hand,
needed time to process and felt stifled by Jamal's reassurance seeking.
He went on long drives to get some fresh air and to self-soothe, which
felt to Jamal like further abandonment. Despite their mutual sadness,
they weren't coming together to lift one another up.*

*Eventually, they were able to reconnect with their mutual
admiration and give one another the benefit of the doubt. Jack was
able to share his fear that he would be stuck with the lion's share of
the parenting while Jamal wrestled with his OCD. Jamal shared that
he knew he needed to work on exposures again but was too ashamed
to spend money on more therapy when they were funneling it into the
adoption. The couple worked through this difficult situation with
patience and mutual respect, recognizing that they had a common
goal to minimize the effect of Jamal's OCD.*

You can work through your issues in partnership too. The first step is
clarifying your values, as you did around friendship in chapter 4. This
time you'll explore your values in romantic relationships.

Romantic Partnership: *Exploring Your Values*

Imagine finding a pair of odd sunglasses with neon lines shooting across the
frames. As you lift them to your face, you're transported back to your happiest
memory with a romantic partner. It's as though you've traveled back in time to

this moment and are inhabiting your body again. What are you doing together? Where are you? What are you feeling in this moment with your loved one? How do they make you feel and how do you hope that you're making them feel? See if you can sink into this moment for a while and immerse yourself in the sights, sounds, tastes, smells, and physical sensations. Then write down any value words that describe this experience (you may want to refer back to the list of values in chapter 4). You may do this for more than one experience if you like and collect a few value words to use for relationship exposures.

Next you'll use the same technique that you used in chapter 4: building an exposure hierarchy by identifying the discrepancies between what you would like to do if living by your values in a relationship and what OCD currently allows you to do.

When Jamal examined his romantic values, he found himself transported back to the moment that Jack met his parents and siblings. Seeing the man he loved integrated into his family brought him joy and a sense of wholeness. He felt profoundly connected at this time, both to Jack and to his family, and so he chose "connectedness" as one of his values. He was able to use this as a springboard to come up with relationship exposures that would both challenge OCD and increase his connectedness to Jack. He selected engaging with the adoption process again and resuming their weekly walks, which led them past a busy playground, as initial exposure targets.

Value	Romantic Relationship Exposure	Willingness
Connectedness	Start doing adoption tasks together	9
Connectedness	Resume weekly walks together (past nearby playground)	6

To strengthen your romantic relationships against the interference of OCD symptoms, use the "Romantic Relationships Exposure Hierarchy" available at http://www.newharbinger.com/50584. First review your list of values in relationships, and choose three to five values that describe how you want to be as a romantic partner. Write these values at the top of the worksheet. In the first column, list those values that you want to express but currently avoid. Then in the second column, write down some activities that you'd like to be able to do with your partner to express these values. In the third column, rate each activity on a scale of 1 to 10 to indicate how willing you are to try it, where 1 indicates that you're definitely unwilling to try this exposure now and 10 means that you're willing to jump in as soon as possible And get going!

Having and Holding

Although this chapter only touches on some of the ways that OCD can impact your love life, I hope that it has provided some tools to get you closer to your relationship goals. If you're single, I hope that you feel confident knowing that you're lovable and worthy of building a partnership that is profoundly gratifying. If you're partnered, I want you to see the possibilities in the relationship beyond what OCD lets you see right now. Now, for the next chapter, you might want to slip into something more comfortable...as we'll be talking about OCD and sex.

CHAPTER 6

In the Bedroom
Sexual Intimacy and OCD

Many people with OCD say that they live from the neck up, spending hours chasing thoughts around their heads without resolution. Living in your thoughts in this way can detach you from your sensory experience of the world and from the very body that carries you through it. Others with OCD will wince when asked about their relationship with their bodies. Perhaps sensorimotor OCD symptoms have made your body feel like an enemy, full of jarring sensations and feelings of not-quite-rightness. Or contamination symptoms have rendered your natural bodily fluids and odors a source of disgust. If you have health anxiety, you may be overly attentive to your body's natural fluctuations, and if you have SO-OCD, you may be threatened by an inopportune rush of blood to your groin. But the good news is that having OCD doesn't necessarily mean having an indifferent or antagonistic relationship with your body. You can learn to explore your capacity for pleasure even if anxiety, urges, and intrusive thoughts come along for the journey. And you can learn to explore and enjoy other peoples' bodies too.

Admittedly, I was more nervous about writing this chapter than any other. Sexual health and satisfaction are such broad topics, and I wanted to be deliberate about affirming different sexual orientations and preferences as well as the diverse values that people associate with sex. To this end, I'm using the word "sex" broadly for any consensual behavior with another person that causes arousal. It need not be penetrative or lead to climax, and it certainly doesn't have to occur within a heterosexual monogamous relationship. You may view sex as a way to deepen strong emotional connections and you may see it as a vehicle to explore dynamics of power and play. You may see sex as a sacred act limited to married people or you may see it as a means of artful self-expression. Whoever you are and whoever your partners are, I hope that this chapter is helpful in outlining and addressing the ways that OCD impacts sex. We'll discuss sexual identity development, the impact of OCD on arousal, common ways that OCD can present in sex, and how to apply principles from sex therapy to enhance your sexual experiences. Please note that past sexual trauma can have a considerable impact on the way that you experience sexual intimacy. If this is part of your history, consider working with a therapist to help disentangle some of those effects and to make sure that you feel safe, empowered, and present in your body.

Your Sexual Identity Development

We all grow up hearing different messages about sexuality. These messages can come from our family, our friends, our community, and the media, to name a few. Even silence around sexuality can impact us, leading to misinformation or shame. As we get older, we begin to internalize some of these messages and incorporate them into our own beliefs. Our thoughts about things like erotic pleasure, desirability, the morality of sex, and the gender roles we're often told we must fulfill begin to coalesce in adolescence, just as our hormones infuse us with a healthy dose of desire. This is both an exciting and a confusing time. How is anyone supposed to feel comfortable about sex among the chaos of sprouting hair, flashes of lust, and strong cultural messages? What happens in this time can influence our stance toward and experience of sex and intimacy for years to come—especially when you add OCD symptoms to the mix.

What You Heard: *Recalling Early Messages*

Reflect on your early messages about sex. Did you learn about sex and sexuality at school, at home, from faith leaders, from movies, or from pornography? When sex was brought up in your family, was it a welcome topic or a record-scratch moment? What emotions were associated with sex: joy, anxiety, shame, guilt? How much do you believe those messages now? Grab a pencil and paper and write down whatever comes to mind in response to these questions. Or you can use the "Messages About Sex" worksheet, available at http://www.newharbinger.com/50584. Reflecting on these early messages may help you identify some thoughts that interact with your OCD to hinder your experience of sex.

Research shows that access to comprehensive sex education—that is, education that provides unbiased information about sex and sexuality and promotes personal choice—is associated with lower levels of distress about sex, lower levels of sexually transmitted infections, and reduced likelihood of sexual assault later in life (MacDowall et al. 2015). This doesn't mean that any one set of values about sex is superior to others, but it does suggest that having choice and autonomy in exploring your sexuality is a good thing. Given that OCD often attaches itself to taboo topics and themes, it may also mean that people who have restricted access to information about sex are at increased risk of having intrusive thoughts about sex. It's basically like telling a child not to touch a big shiny button and then inundating her with opportunities to touch big shiny buttons.

The point at which you first developed OCD symptoms may also have an impact on your beliefs about sex or sexual behavior. Some people who first experienced symptoms in childhood or early adolescence say that after their OCD symptoms became quieter with treatment, they felt freer to explore their sexuality without the specters of harm worries, contamination concerns, or moral scrupulosity. In this way, it's possible to experience a second puberty of sorts, a time in which to clarify your desires, attractions, and beliefs about sex and sexuality. If you've found yourself at this crossroads, remember that it's never too late to explore the wonderful ways that your body can experience pleasure with others.

Research on Human Sexuality

Sex therapy is a relatively new field, and we still have much to learn about human sexuality. For years, psychological theories of sex featured the ideas of Sigmund Freud, a man who, among other harmful beliefs, thought that women who were unable to experience orgasms from vaginal penetration were sexually immature. He also chalked up much of sexual development to people's feelings about their parents, which indicates that he had an exceedingly active imagination, extremely hot parents, or both. Outside of psychology, the state of sexual science was grim as well. For example, the anatomy of the clitoris, an organ integral to the sexual pleasure of about half of the population, wasn't fully explored until the late 1990s. At a time when we had visited the moon multiple times and discovered ice on a remote moon of Jupiter, science was still struggling to understand things much closer to home.

In the 1960s, research on human sexuality saw a breakthrough with the work of William Masters and Virginia Johnson, two researchers who studied patterns of arousal in hundreds of people and developed a four-stage model of sexual response. This model stated that sexual response progressed in a linear fashion; that is, that each stage was dependent on the one before it. When stimulated, you start with the excitement stage and progress to plateau, orgasm, and resolution stages. Masters and Johnson also discussed the role of anxiety in inhibiting sexual response. They introduced the term *spectatoring*, which is when people get so caught up in viewing and judging their own and their partner's performance that they lose touch with the sensations that maintain arousal. If you fit in the "living above the neck" category, this may resonate as a cause of sexual performance anxiety.

Masters and Johnson proposed using a technique called *sensate focus* to help bring people back into contact with their sensory experiences of themselves and their partners. Sensate focusing is a way of using physical touch to explore your partner's body without the expectation or pressures of sex (Masters and Johnson 1970). I'll talk more about it later in the chapter and provide an activity that combines sensate focus with mindfulness.

While the work of Masters and Johnson was helpful for a basic understanding of arousal patterns, it focused solely on the physical aspects of sexual responsiveness, failing to capture psychological aspects which can make things more complex. Additionally, most of the participants in their studies were white, middle-class, married couples—hardly representative of the sexual experiences of everyone. Newer models of sexual response have strayed from the linear model to adopt more of a cyclical one, in which desire can occur with or without direct stimulation and in which desire and emotional intimacy can influence each other. Put another way, if you feel loved and cared for by your partner, you're more likely to have satisfying sex, which in turn leads you to feel more loved. Rinse and repeat. One such model acknowledges the psychological and emotional components of sexual response while recognizing that orgasm need not be central to sex (Basson et al. 2004). Some sex therapy researchers have noted that including psychological aspects of arousal in models may be especially relevant to cisgender women who may have different motivations for partnered sex than cisgender men (speaking broadly, of course). Currently, there's little research that explores sexual response in transgender, gender nonconforming, and intersex people, but fortunately, sexuality experts are at work formulating trans-inclusive models. With how new this field is, suffice it to say that we still have a lot left to learn about sex.

In her influential 2015 book, *Come as You Are*, Dr. Emily Nagoski lays out the two factors at play in our experience of desire: the sexual excitation system and the sexual inhibitory system, or as she succinctly puts it, the "accelerator" and the "brakes." The accelerator is what gets us going sexually. It's our brain's ability to find and pay attention to all the sexy things in the world, including our own arousing thoughts. The brakes, on the other hand, slow down or halt the process of arousal. (*You could get an STI!* Brake. *You just thought about your grandpa's scrotum!* Brake. *You're not going to perform as well as his past partners!* Brake.) Everyone falls on a spectrum within these two systems. While some people require lots of stimulation and fantasy to get even a little aroused (low accelerator), others need only a breeze across their neck to feel desire (high accelerator). Also, while some people can stay aroused easily in the face of unsexy thoughts or sensations (low brakes), others have internal alarm bells and external cues that can bring the Sexmobile to a screeching halt easily (high brakes). Moreover, as you can imagine, OCD has something to say about both our accelerator and our brakes.

Savannah's Story

When Savannah got her period at age ten, her mother discouraged her from using tampons, telling her that they would be painful with her petite frame. At her all-girls Catholic school, Savannah received abstinence-only sex education and limited information about menstruation other than how to stay "hygienic." Throughout adolescence and early adulthood, Savannah continued using pads, concerned that inserting anything into her vagina would hurt. She was devoted to her studies and didn't date much in high school or college. She began dating her first serious boyfriend, Connor, when she was twenty-three years old. When Connor wanted to touch her genitals, Savannah stopped him, letting him know that she wasn't ready for that. He was understanding, and she engaged in manual and oral stimulation of his penis so that they could have a sexual relationship. While she wanted to please him, she also began to feel a discrepancy in their relationship, and her resentment about this difference grew over time.

About five months in, Savannah experienced her first OCD symptoms. She was gripped by contamination worries and emetophobia *(fear of vomiting)*. Her contamination fears centered around contracting scabies, a skin condition caused by an infestation of mites burrowing into the skin. She began changing her clothing every time she got home and frequently checked her skin for signs of itchiness or redness. Her fears bled into her interactions with Connor, whose body she inspected thoroughly before touching or kissing him and who had to change into "safe" clothing whenever he visited. He was confused but willing to comply with these requests to help her feel more comfortable. One day, she went down on him and gagged as his penis touched the back of her throat. She burst into tears, panicking that she would throw up, and pushed him away from her. He became angry, yelling that he was trying his best to be clean enough for her, only to be told that he made her want to vomit. Fueled by both her OCD and her frustration about their sex life, she broke up with him. Shortly thereafter, she sought treatment and received an OCD diagnosis.

In session, it was clear that Savannah hadn't really wanted to break up with Connor; she loved him deeply but felt resentful of their sexual mismatch and ashamed about having what she imagined was an abnormally small vagina. Once her OCD had begun labeling physical touch as a possible risk, she became exhausted with the rituals she needed to complete before intimacy. With encouragement in therapy, she expressed her concerns to a gynecologist and found out that her vagina was average in size. She gradually began using progressively larger tampons, and when she experienced no pain, her fear of sexual penetration also decreased. Through ERP, she confronted her fears of scabies and vomiting while reducing her compulsions of excessive washing and changing clothes. Finally, she learned some assertiveness skills to advocate for herself sexually and to navigate consent, as she became more interested in being touched and having sex. Connor was open to reconciling with Savannah once the circumstances behind the breakup were clear, and as Savannah was able to be more open with him about her OCD, he began to *understand the context for her compulsions and learned how to best support her.*

This example deliberately contains information about how early sex education and cultural messages can combine with OCD symptoms to create difficulties or dissatisfaction with sex. Savannah is not alone in having experienced shame, anxiety, and misinformation about her body, and when it came to her sex life, the onset of OCD complicated the picture for her even further. In my experience, many clients come into therapy with anxiety or discomfort around sex that's separate from the influence of their OCD. While those in more sexually conservative cultures may have less information and more shame, those in the LGBTQIA+ community must contend with external messages about the very legitimacy or morality of their genders or sexualities.

Finally, I want to add that you've likely learned much that is positive and helpful along with other messages that may make sex harder or more challenging. Be sure to acknowledge the ways your history and life experience have provided insight that empowers you, even as you acknowledge and confront the challenges you might be facing.

How OCD Affects Arousal

Research shows that people with OCD experience higher levels of *anorgasmia* (inability to orgasm), lower sexual satisfaction, lower desire, decreased positivity of sexual thoughts, and lower arousal than people who don't have OCD (Koolwal et al. 2020). Certain medications that people with OCD may take to manage symptoms—for example, selective serotonin reuptake inhibitors (SSRIs)—can further lower desire, making you less sensitive to sexual stimulation both mental and physical. OCD symptoms themselves can attack sex in a variety of ways, making intimacy feel less about pleasure and more about risk. If OCD has caused you trouble with sex, please know that you're not alone in your struggles and that it's not your fault. Fortunately, as sex therapy and OCD treatment have rapidly advanced over the past thirty years, so have our methods to help people cultivate rich and satisfying sexual relationships.

Remember the accelerator and brakes analogy? OCD can interfere with both systems, leading to frustration about sexual functioning. Higher levels of anxiety make for stronger brakes, meaning that the more anxious you are, the less you can access your arousal. This comes up in two main ways: fears about the outcomes of sex and fears about sexual performance. OCD-related fears about the outcomes of sex may look like worries about getting pregnant, contracting a disease, physically harming your partner, challenging your sexual orientation, or proving that you're sexually deviant for having certain thoughts during intimacy (spoiler: you're not!). Fears about performance may also arise with SO-OCD or harm themes, especially if your OCD tells you that you must perform well to show how much you really fancy your partner (and not, say, your cousin, as your obsessions may claim). ROCD loves performance fears and can ruin a perfectly good moment of intimacy with demands that you *feel perfectly aroused and in tune* throughout sex. Anxiety also has a paradoxical effect on orgasm. That is, if you're trying to prolong your orgasm, you may have one sooner, and if you're trying hard to get there, it may be elusive.

Consider how your OCD affects your arousal. Does OCD make it more elusive or inconsistent? You can practice accepting the existence of your thoughts and feelings, and bringing your attention back to the present when you feel yourself pulled away. Moreover, you can maintain clear communication with partners, so you can work together to make sex a mutually enjoyable experience. We will return to the topics of how to use mindfulness and communication to enhance sex, but first let's take a closer look at some OCD symptoms that tend to get in the way and how you can respond to them.

Contamination Symptoms

Contamination fears are a common barrier to comfort with sex, and they tend to come in one of two varieties: danger or disgust. Some people with contamination OCD worry about contracting an STI, getting another illness, accidentally ingesting fecal matter, becoming pregnant, causing pregnancy, or contaminating an otherwise clean surface with dangerous fluids. Others worry about the messiness of sex. There's saliva, sweat, vaginal secretions, and semen, not to mention the odors, textures, tastes, and sounds that accompany sexual acts. Contamination symptoms can affect sexual intimacy by associating these natural bodily processes with disgust. And it's not just human triggers: condoms smell funny, lube is sticky, and the squeak of latex may set your teeth on edge.

The curious thing about disgust is that it can be a moral emotion as well. Think about something that you find unconscionable and you may find your face curling into the same grimace that it does when you see something gross. If you've been taught to associate certain sexual thoughts with immorality, then sex can seem like a (literally) slippery slope to acts of violence or depravity. In American culture, for example, the word "dirty" is often used for certain sexual behaviors. This can enhance arousal for some who feel that the hidden and therefore taboo nature of sex increases its desirability. But for others who struggle with contamination fears, the concept of engaging in "dirty" acts may feel threatening or humiliating. It's important to think about the language that works best for you and to communicate this to your partner.

Scrupulosity and Sex

Morality and sex are intricately intertwined in many cultures, and OCD can hijack these customs and values, turning sex into a scrupulosity minefield. For example, in the Orthodox Jewish faith, wives take monthly trips to a purifying bath, or *mikvah*, after their menstrual period ends and abstain from sex with their husbands during this interval. While this is an important part of religious ritual, it can easily be commandeered by OCD as a target of compulsions; women may worry that they haven't properly cleansed themselves or perfectly recited their prayers, or they may repeatedly check themselves before the bath to ensure that their period is over. When having sex with their partners, they may experience divided attention or reduced arousal as a result of scrupulosity concerns. They may also go out of their way to avoid anything arousing during the time between menstruating and purification, fearing that they'll lose control and seek out sex. All of this can create an association between sex and anxiety, further impairing intimacy. Customs and beliefs from other religions can also be appropriated by OCD to fuel scrupulosity around sex. For example, some Christians may worry that having sexual thoughts about people other than their spouse is akin to committing adultery and may confess compulsively. Some Muslims may have scrupulosity related to purification rituals that are performed after menstruation or ejaculation.

Scrupulosity need not be religious for it to affect sex. Other moral systems can make an appearance during intimacy. Perhaps your OCD is chastising you for allowing your mind to wander (as if we have control!) to that handsome coworker while having sex with your partner. You may feel a rush of guilt about this thought, particularly if you find your arousal increasing. While OCD may equate your wandering thoughts to cheating, the only thing you're guilty of is having a perfectly normal brain and an attractive colleague. The good news is that it's possible to adhere to religious or moral codes without letting OCD call the shots. Consider what your values tell you and then consider if OCD is adding a little off-color flavor to the mix. If OCD's spin on things is inconsistent with what you want, refocus on the here and now.

Intrusive Thoughts and Sensations

Given that our minds like to wander, it's not surprising that many people (with or without OCD) report unwanted thoughts during sex. While these can feel like odd mental blips to those who don't struggle with OCD, they can feel devastating for those who do. Your OCD may try to tell you that these bizarre, taboo, violent, or otherwise uncomfortable thoughts reflect your character or values, but they absolutely don't. Even so, the idea of allowing intrusive thoughts to be there may feel abhorrent or irresponsible. Please be kind to yourself if you're experiencing this. Your mind and your body aren't always on the same page, and feeling aroused by your partner's touch while unsavory images play in your head doesn't necessarily mean that the images are significant in your arousal.

A few years ago, I worked with a young adult who accidentally walked in on his younger brother's best friend undressing in the family bathroom. The image of this child's "junk" was burned into his mind. "It just keeps popping up and I can't help it!" he exclaimed. "I feel like I'm going to be having sex with my girlfriend, and boom! I see that kid's junk!" When something like this happens, it's a good idea to try taking it lightly, with humor. My client practiced imagining the worst—the junk following him everywhere around the house—and yelling "Boom! That kid's junk!" at random times. Humor helped to create distance between the symptom and his negative interpretation of its meaning. And so, when it did pop up in the middle of sex, he was better able to shrug it off and come back to the present.

This phenomenon of your mind and body being on two different pages is so common that it has its own name, *arousal nonconcordance*. This is what happens when your genitals are experiencing arousal but your mind is not, which those in the OCD community like to refer to as "groinals" (see discussion chapter 3). These unwanted sensations are often used by OCD as a marker of true arousal when in fact they're just bodies doing their thing. For example, if someone with pedophilia-themed OCD (POCD) feels arousal after playing with a child, they may see this as evidence that they're sexually attracted to kids, but in reality, the simple act of scanning your body for arousal or mentally worrying about arousal can cause these sensations. As an example, do you have to pee right now? Chances are that when I asked that, you suddenly realized you did. You're welcome.

Cultivating Curiosity with Your Partner

If there's one thing that OCD absolutely hates, it's the idea of curiosity about uncertain or ambiguous events. With OCD, deviations from plans can feel like harbingers of doom. Your mind and body must color within the lines, acting in ways that are predictable, rational, and according to plan. But good sexual intimacy often requires a fair bit of spontaneity. Bodies react to novelty, which is the sole reason why *Cosmopolitan* magazine can run yet another version of the story "20 New Ways to Spice Up Your Love Life" every year. But cultivating curiosity with OCD is difficult, because anxiety and disgust can shut it down. Here are some ways to quell these emotions and bring curiosity back into your sex life.

Getting to Know Your Body

Education about our bodies, sexuality, and sexual practices is one way to reduce disgust and fear around bodily fluids, textures, and odors. In a recent study, people with OCD looked at pictures of food along with videos of people vomiting, and over time, the food pictures began to evoke disgust by association, a process we call *conditioning*. However, when those in the study were given the chance to think about vomiting as a positive act of ridding the body of harmful substances, their disgust ratings fell for both the food pictures and the vomiting videos (Olatunji et al. 2017). Said another way, changing your beliefs about things that OCD has labeled as gross can help to reduce feelings of disgust over them.

When it comes to sex, if your OCD labels natural bodily processes or parts as disgusting, you can work on acknowledging what's wonderful about your own or your partner's body. How magical is it that semen houses one-half of what's needed to create a new human life? That the vagina is a self-cleaning wonder nestled under intricate folds? That we sweat to regulate our temperature? Learning to appreciate what OCD tells you is disgusting can help minimize those feelings of disgust so that you can explore your body with your partner without those feelings getting in the way.

Identifying and Eliminating Compulsions

Although exposure gets most of the attention in ERP, using response prevention consistently is the most effective way to cut OCD off at the source (no scratching, no itching). And sex is no exception: identifying and eliminating your compulsions around sex can be crucial in reducing symptoms and increasing your capacity to be present. Below is a list of common compulsions associated with sex. You may want to jot down any in your journal that apply to you:

- Using pornography to check for sensations of arousal or to clarify sexual attraction to certain genders or sex acts

- Engaging in sex to test your sexual orientation or functioning or to confirm a partner's desire for you

- Taking sexual enhancement drugs such as Viagra to ensure that your performance will be adequate or "just in case" a sexual encounter may occur

- Masturbating to attain a "just right" feeling before completing other tasks

- Inserting objects into your vagina, anus, or urethra to test for sensations of pleasure or to provide confirmation of sexual preferences

Avoidance often works like a compulsion as well. That is, if you avoid things that you worry may trigger your symptoms, you're sending the message to your brain that these things are indeed dangerous. Further, avoidance can stifle your ability to try novel sexual activities. For example, a heterosexual man with SO-OCD may be resistant to trying pegging (anal penetration with a strap-on dildo) with his partner because of fears that enjoying the act might "confirm" his worries of being gay. Someone with harm OCD may be reluctant to explore their interest in dominance and submission out of worries about bondage leading to nonconsensual or harmful acts.

This kind of thinking flies in the face of what we know about fantasy and fetish, which is that we can be turned on by all kinds of things that carry little to no meaning outside of our arousal! Having domination fantasies doesn't mean you're violent, and thinking about other people during sex doesn't mean that you're likely to leave your partner. Of course, it's important to remember that you may not want to engage in certain sexual acts due to a myriad of non-OCD reasons! It's perfectly normal to have more conventional tastes in the bedroom or to find that a particular act or technique your partner wants to try just doesn't appeal to you. However, if fear is a primary motivation to avoid what would otherwise be a curious or fun exploration, then consider that this could be another area of exposure.

Being Present

While some OCD therapists treat sexual fears the same way that they approach traditional exposure therapy—gradually completing increasingly difficult sex acts and waiting for anxiety to decline—this runs the risk of just white-knuckling your way through different acts with the goal of getting through them and, in the process, squashing your desire. If we know that anxiety makes arousal more difficult, then taking a purely exposure-based approach is likely to make sex less rather than more enjoyable. Another approach that's grounded in research about our sexual responsiveness is to use a combination of sensate focus and mindfulness-based techniques to enhance your experience of sex and stay connected with your partner and your body throughout intimacy.

As discussed earlier in the chapter, sensate focus is a technique where you engage in nonsexual touch with your partner without the goal of sexual arousal or orgasm. The idea is to explore each other's bodies as if you were experiencing it for the first time, with all the curiosity and wonder that goes along with this novelty. Because there aren't any sexual goals, sensate focus allows you to shed expectations of how this touch will feel and to curb judgments about your own or your partner's responses. Sensate focus happens in phases. You can try it in the next exercise.

Try This: *Sensate Focusing*

Get comfortable with your partner. You can be completely naked or wearing undergarments. In the first phase, for fifteen minutes take turns touching each other in all areas other than the chest or breasts and genitals. As you are being touched, observe any sensations as they arise, focusing on temperature, texture, and pressure as focal points for mindful awareness. Trade off this experience with your partner so that each of you gets to focus on the experience of being touched and touching. Now move on to touching the genitals and chest or breasts, still with a focus on awareness rather than arousal. If arousal arises spontaneously, refrain from engaging in sex. Next, continue with touching, and eventually, if both of you feel ready, you can engage in sensual penetration while attending nonjudgmentally to the sensations that arise.

More recently, mindfulness-based sex therapy research has shown promise for all kinds of people, including those with sexual pain, erectile unpredictability, and reduced sensation following surgery. This list of questions from Dr. Lori Brotto's book, *Better Sex Through Mindfulness* (2018), can help gently steer your awareness while you're intimate with your partner:

What patterns of color, shape, or movement do you see as you look at your partner?

At the points of contact between you and your partner, what temperature/pressure/sensation do you experience?

Do you notice sensations of movement, such as expansion/stretching/contraction in those parts of your body where you are making voluntary movements?

What are the individual sounds that you hear as you breathe? Listen to your partner and notice any sounds. What do you hear when you vocalize? (189)

With OCD, mindfulness as applied to sexual intimacy can serve as an anchor in the body when your mind roams into the territory of obsessions. Try it out.

Getting It On

If sex has become a chore for you or if OCD has layered it with anxiety, fear, or disgust, your experience is like that of many others. But using ERP and mindfulness to reinvigorate your sex life with spontaneity, playfulness, and curiosity will help you connect with your partner or partners despite OCD's protests.

CHAPTER 7

Moving In
Roommates and Partners at Home

Moving in and sharing a living space with someone can be a challenge, and this is especially true when you have OCD. Scores of posts and blogs by people with OCD talk about how scary and frustrating it can be to share space with others. And posts reflecting the other side of the issue talk about how challenging it can be having a roommate with OCD. Even when you don't have OCD, moving in with people can feel like solving a math equations full of complex calculations and tedious steps. How do you manage the practical aspects of cohabitation, such as sharing the bathroom or splitting utility costs? What about making decisions about décor or the frequency of parties? How freely can you pass gas around each other?

When you have OCD, the OCD itself becomes an additional variable in the equation. It's a variable that keeps changing, throwing off all your previous work when a new symptom pops up. Each time OCD shifts, you stop and recalculate, considering what *your anxiety* demands that you do, what *you* truly want to do, and what *the other people* in the home need so they can feel comfortable too. If you've ever been in this situation or if you're encountering it now, I hope that this chapter provides validation that merging lives in a shared physical space can feel overwhelming. And, more importantly, that there are ways to work through it and cultivate fulfilling cohabitation relationships. In this chapter, we'll discuss some of the common ways that OCD gets in the way at home as well as how to address it with housemates and partners through the clarification of roles, negotiation of shared spaces, assertive communication, and disclosure when appropriate.

OCD at Home

Many of us first experience OCD symptoms in childhood and see how it affects (and is affected by) living with others while we're still growing up. It's estimated that over half of people with OCD begin experiencing symptoms before age eighteen (Geller, Homayoun, and Johnson 2021). This means that OCD is an invisible roommate living with us along with our other family members. When we're young, our family members may even notice our OCD symptoms before we have the language to label them ourselves, and how they respond to our symptoms can set the stage for what we come to expect from others when moving in together later on in life.

If our family was sensitive and validating while refraining from excessive accommodation of OCD, our early experience of living with others can be positive. However, if we were used to our family members reacting unhelpfully to our symptoms, it can be detrimental. If your parents and guardians were highly accommodating, you may have difficulty later on believing that you are independent enough to function outside of the family system or with new people. You might have had a hard time moving out or trusting yourself to connect with others. If your family was dismissive or punishing, you may have guilt or shame about bringing your symptoms into a new home with others. You might be especially hesitant to disclose your symptoms and might avoid sharing space because of worries about possible rejection or conflict.

Sometimes OCD takes its sweet time, and symptoms first appear in adulthood. In this case, you may already be living independently or alongside a roommate or partner when it arises. Your behaviors can change in real time for you and others living in the home, creating confusion or arguments. You may find yourself concerned with maintaining the house as a clean, safe, or orderly environment, much to the chagrin of your laid-back partner. Or you may develop disturbing thoughts and withdraw from others, confusing your gregarious housemates. On top of this, if it takes a while to get a diagnosis, you may also be just as befuddled as your housemates as you struggle without a clear explanation for your behavior.

Regardless of your previous experiences of OCD in the home, each new day is another chance to build your relationships with housemates, partners, and others. Along with them, you can cocreate the kind of home environment and relationships that help you feel secure, without letting OCD rule the roost.

Recognizing Roles and Responsibilities

Each home is a mini society with a mini economy. And, as you and others in the home are aware, household currencies extend beyond money. Cleaning the cat's litter box, changing the water filter, and sweeping the kitchen all count as important contributions and may have different values to different people. In my home, for example, doing the laundry is a relatively "expensive" task for my husband, who dislikes all the sorting and folding. I, on the other hand, find the whole process to be an exercise in mindfulness, so it's low cost to me. Alternatively, he doesn't mind washing the dishes after a large meal, while I find scraping food off pans infuriating. Identifying tasks that are inexpensive for one person and expensive to others is a great way to divide up labor in the house. But since I've yet to meet someone who loves scrubbing the toilet, there are bound to be some responsibilities that must be shared. Sitting down with others in your home and figuring out who can do which tasks can make the transition to living together smoother and prevent later conflicts about chores—important not only for the household economy but also for your relationships.

When OCD enters the picture, however, the whole calculus of household labor can get thrown off! Maybe you didn't mind checking the mailbox before your OCD told you that mail is contaminated, or you only avoid cutting the lawn because of intrusive harm thoughts. You know that avoiding these tasks is a direct result of OCD, but you still feel paralyzed when thinking about them. Unfortunately, the actions that feel the costliest may also be the best for your recovery. This can be a point of frustration and shame, but it's an OC-normal part of your recovery: seeing that doing uncomfortable things in the short term is a way to reduce your pain in the long run. And remember that you can ease into tasks that are difficult instead of jumping into the deep end. You can choose progressively more challenging exposure tasks that allow you to edge toward taking responsibilities in a feared area. Doing so helps to reestablish balance in the living space and reduce the likelihood of resentment from (or indebtedness to) others. If you're ready and willing to inform others in the home about your OCD, you may also gain some supportive allies who can participate in your exposures or cheer you on.

If, for example, your OCD says that picking up after your dog requires lengthy handwashing in scalding water, you have a few options to choose from:

1. Delegate poop patrol to other pet parents and avoid it altogether.

2. Reluctantly take care of it and continue to have chapped skin.

3. Find a way to split the responsibility somehow until you're ready to take it over as a full exposure.

Can you guess which one of these options wins my vote? Gradual exposure! Maybe you and your partner walk the dog together, and while they continue to do the scooping, you hold the leash and make sure not to look away during the process. Then you practice standing progressively closer to the poop or touching the top of the bag to chuck it in the garbage. The key is to work toward completing the task while refraining from doing your compulsions according to OCD's rules afterward. That means the work extends to when you get home and feel compelled to do a rigorous and painful handwash. Doing a quick handwash in comfortably cool water is the final power move against your OCD. And if doing that is too hard at first, you can break it down into steps too. Use less soap, decrease the time it takes to wash, or use warm water. As you take more ownership of different tasks, this shows others in your home that you're chipping away at OCD's rules about what you can and can't do. Your housemates, family members, or partner will see that you're moving toward a more equitable delegation of responsibilities.

USING ERP TO ACCOMPLISH HOUSEHOLD GOALS

You can create an ERP plan to conquer your chore-related worries and improve the balance of labor in your home. It's a way to work backwards: going from figuring out what you'd ultimately like to do and coming up with steps to get there. Use the "Setting Household Goals" worksheet at http://www.newharbinger.com/50584.

First, write down a goal behavior and the compulsions or safety behaviors that get in the way when you perform this chore. Remember that compulsions and safety behaviors are any alterations you make in how you do something to lower your anxiety. These are things that go above and beyond what a person without OCD would do. For example, wearing gloves when you cut jalapeños isn't necessarily compulsive, even though many people choose not to do it (just ask my eyes after I rub them on taco night!). However, if you're wearing gloves to cut other vegetables, this could be a compulsion or safety behavior. You want to aim for doing exposures that will allow you to resist compulsions and safety behaviors associated with these actions. If you're not sure about what your compulsions would be in a particular case, because you've been avoiding the goal task altogether, that's okay too; just write down any compulsions that you suspect would come up. Here's an example of how to set a household goal with ERP:

Goal: Cooking a meal

Associated compulsions/safety behaviors: Excessive stove checking; having another person in the room for reassurance; putting all knives away

Possible exposure steps:

1. Help to cook a meal with roommate by doing tasks that don't involve chopping or stovetop use (measuring ingredients, reading the recipe, washing the vegetables).

2. Help to cook as in previous exposure but do so while hanging out next to the knives.

3. Cook something with roommate that involves chopping but no stovetop use.

4. Cook something with roommate that involves stovetop use but no chopping.

5. Make a meal that involves chopping and using the stovetop with room-mate in the kitchen.

6. Make a meal that involves chopping and using the stovetop without anyone else in the kitchen.

It's okay and even positive to get creative here! If there are certain knives that are scarier to OCD than others, you can even integrate in a hierarchy of knives from dullest to sharpest. There's no right or wrong way to make strides toward your ultimate goal, as long as you're pushing yourself closer to this sense of equity with others. And be sure to keep an eye on those sneaky compulsions. If you do your exposures but still end up checking the stove repeatedly, you've just given your OCD more power! Make sure that you're chipping away at your use of compulsions as you progress.

Sharing Physical Spaces in Harmony

When you think about your home, its rooms, hallways, and outdoor areas, which parts have been colonized by the whims of OCD? Do you have any areas that must be kept *just so* or any that have been deemed off-limits to you or anyone else in your home? If so, it's time to think of these places as your battlegrounds in the fight to reclaim territory from OCD. Remember, it's your home: the one place that you can go to rest, recharge, and cultivate as your own. You ought to have that. And while OCD tells you that the only way to appreciate your home is to follow all of its rules, the opposite is true. The more rules you follow, the more rules OCD will generate, leaving you feeling like you're paying compulsion tolls at every turn to just enjoy your space. What's more, when your house-mates don't understand these invisible rules, they may break them repeatedly, leaving at least one and maybe both of you frustrated.

If you're shaking your head and saying to yourself that your home is actually the one place that feels free of certain rituals or rules, I get that. Maybe it feels like you get home and finally unwind, away from the triggers of the outside world. Maybe so…but like a third grader dropping the "Santa isn't real" bomb, I'm here to challenge that view. You may feel like your home is a respite precisely because you can carve out the space to comply with OCD's wishes. This isn't freedom; it's creating a fertile environment for symptoms to grow and amplify. If you have worries about contamination, for instance, OCD may demand that your home be clean, pure, or safe. You do your best to achieve this, policing what can and can't cross certain thresholds. Or perhaps you rid your bedroom of triggering items, hiding the picture of you and your ex (whom, because of your harm OCD, you fear you may have assaulted, even though you have no memory of ever harming them) or ridding the shelves of your old books about philosophy (because they remind you that life could be meaningless). While this can feel at first blush like a symptom-free zone, it's truly a stronghold of what I call "OCD Nation," upheld by avoidance.

Those you share space with didn't sign up to live in OCD Nation. They didn't get their passports stamped or read the OCD constitution—which, incidentally, lists OCD as the sole member of the legislative, judicial, and executive branches. They're unlikely to follow its laws, and for good reason: to them, the rules are arbitrary and stifling. And while you feel that too, the rules also feel like a way to keep adversaries of uncertainty, fear, dread, guilt, and disgust at bay. However, just as contributing to the household economy is a part of improving your relationships with others in your domestic orbit, so is freeing your home of these battle-grounds and making spaces more accessible to everyone, including you.

RECLAIMING SPACE BY EVICTING OCD

It can feel overwhelming to think about eliminating the spaces in your home that feel the safest, especially when so many other places in the world evoke anxiety, disgust, and discomfort. You may feel a pit in your stomach just thinking about tackling this. I understand that hesitation but ask that you allow that discomfort to be present without it direct-ing the show. I promise that evicting OCD from your home is both possible and incredibly rewarding, and by doing it slowly, and with support and self-compassion, you can demonstrate to yourself that you're resilient enough to work toward a life without OCD calling the shots. Others in your home may help as well, either by creating natural opportunities to challenge OCD's rules (*Oh, you brought home a rabbit to skin in the kitchen?*) or by providing support as you do the difficult work of reclaiming physical spaces. Mapping out where OCD lives in your home, and how to flush it out, can also be a useful tool.

Okay, by now, you've probably surmised that I don't know much about military strategy. This is true. However, I do feel like an armchair general every time I get my crayons out and help clients make blueprints of the layout of their homes. You can download a sample Floor Plan of Attack at http://www.newharbinger.com/50584. The purpose of this is to identify the areas that are affected by OCD, not those that are affected by appro-priate interpersonal boundaries. That is, if no one else would be allowed in your private bedroom irrespective of OCD, that wouldn't count here.

Floor Plan of Attack: *Mapping Out Where OCD Lives*

Make your own floor plan of attack against OCD in your home. Grab some paper and crayons or colored pencils, and follow these steps:

1. Create a visual of the layout of your living space, including stairways, garages, patios, and anything that can be occupied by OCD. Sketch out each room, including details such as the locations of sinks, toilets, and furniture. Label each room, bedroom, bathroom, and so on. Draw all of this in black or another dark color, as you'll be making multiple copies.

2. Leave a blank spot at the top to write in the date later. This way you can keep track of your progress over time, as you push OCD out of different spaces.

3. At the bottom, make two small boxes and label one "off-limits to me" and the other "off-limits to others." You can add boxes for other rules, depending on how your OCD affects your living space. You'll color in these boxes later to use as your key.

4. Make a few copies of your floor plan, as you'll be using these copies over time to track your progress on multiple fronts of attack.

5. Take a copy of the floor plan, write the date at the top, and choose a color for the areas that are off-limits for you now (or manageable only with compulsions) and another color for areas that are off-limits to others. Color in the corresponding boxes in the key.

6. Now comes the fun part. Using the colors in your key, color in the rooms or areas in the floor plan that are off-limits to you or to others, or to both! Remember: the goal is to identify places that are deemed no-go zones based on OCD. If you don't go into your roommate's room because you've both established a boundary around this, don't color in that room. But if you used to go in there, and OCD then blocked it off, this would be a great "off-limits to me" area.

Use your floor plan, working on your own or with housemates' help, to attack OCD and open up spaces gradually with ERP. Update your floor plans periodically, coloring in new sheets to see how the territory changes. Include the date at the top to see how the map changes over time.

Date:

▢ Off Limits to Me
▨ Off Limits to Others

My clients and I have collaborated to draw many floor plans and sometimes get more creative with our keys. Is this a so-called safe space, determined by OCD to be protected at all costs from any outside contamination? Let's color that blue. The staging area for taking off contaminated clothing? Orange. The kitchen with its meticulous organization system that must not be messed up? Yellow. This rainbow of rules can seem daunting at first, but it's a great way to visualize your goals. Over time, you can update your floor plan with smaller areas of color, watching the margins of OCD's territory shrink.

Standing Up for Yourself

While much of this chapter has been devoted to increasing flexibility and letting go of control in the home, OCD can also lead to a completely different issue: people pleasing. Many people with moral scrupulosity feel a strong desire to keep others happy that goes beyond just being nice.

Maybe you can relate to this. It can look like apologizing multiple times a day and yielding to others' preferences instead of stating your own. You might even feel so guilty that your OCD makes you difficult to live with that you try to ignore your own needs. And this may be yet another sneaky way that OCD's still in charge. It's taking advantage of your tendency toward inflated responsibility.

With inflated responsibility, you try your hardest to prevent conflict or harm at any cost, even when it takes time or attention away from other important things in your life. If you're focused on people pleasing and keeping others happy, you may be neglecting one very important person: yourself! People pleasing can undermine your sense of entitlement to decision making, leading to reduced self-advocacy at home. If this resonates with you, you're not alone. On average, people with OCD show higher rates of submissive behavior in interpersonal relationships than those without mental health concerns (Solem et al. 2015). While there are benefits to being flexible, there are drawbacks as well. Practicing healthy assertiveness in your interactions with your housemates ensures that you have a say in the home. Plus, it's a way of being kind to yourself and reminding yourself that your voice matters even if you have OC-normal struggles. As researcher Kristin Neff (2021) has noted, advocating for yourself is a way of demonstrating self-compassion by taking up the space you deserve to have.

Many people with passive communication styles bristle at the thought of being more assertive, worrying that others will see them as brash, demanding, or domineering. Therefore, it's important to consider the differences between assertive and aggressive communication. Aggressive communication is the battering ram of interpersonal interactions: blunt, unyielding, and designed to get others to bend to its will. With aggressive communication, there's no dialogue about the matter at hand, just a demand hurled by one party at another. Assertiveness, on the other hand, has more breathing room. It's a way of saying "these are my needs" without insisting that the other person change their behavior. It can start a conversation instead of shutting one down. Assertive communication is best used when you want to ask for something or to set a limit with someone. As an example, here's a dialogue between Yuki, a thirty-year-old with OCD, and her roommate Julia. I've added parenthetical commentary to point out some of the ways that Yuki is demonstrating assertiveness.

Yuki: I'd like to talk to you about something apartment related. Is now a good time?

       (By asking Julia about the timing of the conversation, Yuki is demonstrating respect for her roommate and letting her know that this isn't a one-way conversation.)

Julia: Sure, what's up?

Yuki: I've noticed that you're sending me your rent money later and later each month. It feels awkward that I have to keep reminding you too. I know that you're busy, but I wonder if we can find a better system for this so that you can get me the money sooner.

       (Yuki is being direct about her displeasure and clearly asking for a collaborative solution. She also acknowledges that Julia is busy; while not essential, acknowledging that the other person may have some barriers can be helpful.)

Julia: Wow, I guess I didn't think it mattered that much, since I always get it to you before the month is up.

Yuki: It does matter to me. I feel disrespected when it takes that long.

       (Yuki uses an I-message as a way to clearly state her feelings without blaming the other person.)

Julia: I wish you had said something earlier. I had no idea that you were upset, and now I feel awful.

Yuki: I get that. You couldn't have known because I didn't tell you. But
           now that you know, is there a better way to do this?

           *(Yuki might be tempted to apologize at this point, but she stays on
           track. Again, she's offering to help come up with a solution collab-
           oratively here.)*

Julia: I'll set up a monthly reminder on my phone and see if I can set
           it up as a recurring transaction.

Yuki: That sounds great. Thanks for listening to me and for address-
           ing this.

How did it feel to read that interaction? When you think of yourself
being assertive like Yuki did, do you squirm a little bit? If so, you can
think of assertiveness as an exposure task—except, this time, the exposure has the added benefit of helping you get your needs met. Over time,
assertiveness strengthens rather than erodes relationships.

Managing Disclosure in the Home

Sharing space with someone else doesn't mean that you have to share
everything with them. In fact, you may opt not to share anything, and
that's a valid decision. Sometimes this depends on the nature of the relationship. While you may not want to divulge all your symptoms to a new,
unfamiliar roommate, you may find that moving in with a trusted partner
or friend necessitates this level of information sharing. Further, sometimes simply sharing space can reveal things about your symptoms to
others. That is, you may have hidden symptoms from others in a way that
living with a roommate or partner no longer allows. This can feel scary or
invasive, like your behavior is betraying your desire to remain private.

From a deep well of compassion, I offer you a question: would you feel
hesitant to disclose your symptoms if you were struggling with a physical
ailment? For example, if you couldn't have certain lights in the home

because they might trigger migraines, would you feel shame in advocating for yourself about that? If your answer is no, that's understandable. There's far more stigma associated with mental health concerns than those rooted elsewhere in the body. While advocating for yourself doesn't magically make this stigma evaporate, it does allow for you to opt out of reinforcing the stigma, which can be a powerful (and fiercely self-compassionate) move, provided that the person on the receiving end is open to hearing what you have to say.

If you're still unsure about disclosing your symptoms to others, here's another question: if you knew that your roommate or partner were struggling, would you want to know so that you could support them? If so, then you would see their disclosure as an opportunity to understand the context of their behavior and an opportunity to support them in their struggle. If the relationship with others in your house has this level of emotional intimacy and trust, disclosure may be helpful. On the other hand, you may not live with others who will respond with compassion, support, and understanding. If that's the case, then disclosure could cause more rather than less strain in the relationship. Put simply, there are no right or wrong answers to questions about disclosure.

Nelson's Story

When I first met Nelson, he seemed almost physically pained by his symptoms. He'd had OCD symptoms since he was in high school and had received treatment for years. He lived with his parents during college and a few years afterward, working hard to reduce his OCD symptoms. When he moved to Nashville to start a graduate program, Nelson felt confident that living with others would help him build a social network in an unfamiliar city. He was able to find a house with two fellow vegetarians, Leah and June, in a great neighborhood. They cooked together every Sunday, making enough food to last all week, and stayed up late playing board games together. Nelson cared deeply about his roommates, saying that he'd found "chosen family" with them. They were unaware of his OCD and, as far as he could tell, he had no reason to tell them. Then, what he called "the event" happened, and he decided to come to therapy.

Nelson was nervous as he told me about the event, which took place the night of his twenty-fifth birthday. He'd been hanging out with friends at a bar, and he remembered the first part of the night clearly: singing karaoke, buying a round for the table, and flirting with a pretty woman. But he couldn't remember the rest of the night at all. In fact, when Nelson woke up in his bed the next morning, he had no recollection of how he got there—his friends assured him that they'd walked him home—or why he had a tender bruise on his shin. He didn't think much of it at first, as he'd blacked out after drinking before in the past. But then he heard on the local news that a woman's body had been found in a nearby park. She'd been raped, suffocated, and left in a creek. Suddenly, he felt his body go cold. This is probably the girl you were flirting with, he thought. You probably assaulted and killed her, and that's how you got the bruise. You're a dangerous person.

This kind of OCD, sometimes called "false memory OCD," takes advantage of our naturally spotty memory to create and play out some scary what-ifs. As with any other kind of OCD, the compulsions provide only fleeting relief from the worries. Nelson's compulsions included mentally reviewing, scanning the news for updates, seeking reassurance from friends, and researching information about murderers. Leah and June never noticed these compulsions, but they noticed other changes. Overnight, Nelson had gone from a playful and present roommate to a sullen one who spent most of his time in his room. He no longer participated in their Sunday meals and stopped cooking altogether. Their previous arrangement of splitting groceries seemed silly when he was mostly eating takeout, but they still expected him to contribute grocery money based on past arrangements. Nelson's housemates were also upset when he installed a lock on the inside of his room, breaking the landlord's rule about making changes without prior approval. Nelson reasoned that if he was capable of rape and murder under the influence, he might also be dangerous while sleepy. So, he locked himself in every night to prevent sleepwalking into one of the women's rooms and harming them (even without any history of sleepwalking). His roommates tried to talk him about these changes, but he avoided the conversation. He didn't want to bother them with his symptoms and be a burden on them. However, by sidestepping the conversation, he was creating additional stress.

Nelson's OCD had disrupted the economy of their home, and Leah and June had lost him as a friend. Nelson's OCD had also closed him off to huge parts of the home, including both of his roommates' bedrooms, certain parts of the kitchen, the living room, and a shared bathroom.

While Nelson was reluctant to disclose the details of his symptoms to Leah and June, he realized that being honest about his mental health struggles, if not the content of these struggles, would be helpful in repairing his relationship with them. He told his housemates about having OCD and shared which tasks were more difficult for him. He was able to do this because of the foundation of trust on which their relationship was built. Nelson gradually spent more time outside of his room and engaged in values-driven behaviors like joining for board game nights and helping again with cooking. He watched his OCD's territory shrink on his floor plan of attack. Nelson continues to work at chipping away at his OCD symptoms and reports reduced stress from strained relationships at home.

Disclosing to others can greatly benefit your relationships and your home life if your housemates are receptive. Remember that disclosure is always up to you. You don't owe it to others in your home; it's your story and yours alone to share. For more tools to manage disclosure, check out the decisional balance grid in the next chapter too.

The Take-Home Message

Living with others doesn't have to feel impossible when you have OCD. By using ERP techniques to reduce symptoms, advocating for yourself, and collaborating with others in the home, you can ensure that you have happy and respectful relationships with roommates and partners. Now let's shift to the relationships you've had the longest, those with the people who raised you. Put on that ten-year-old reunion T-shirt because we're about to get into managing some of the most difficult relationships of all: those with your family!

CHAPTER 8

We're All in This Together
Family and OCD

Twice monthly I have the honor of welcoming eight brave people into a virtual space and leading an OCD treatment group online. I look forward to this opportunity to encourage clients and, more excitingly, witness them uplifting and supporting one another. Recently, with the holiday season approaching, our group focused on how to prepare for difficulties with symptoms over the holidays. I asked the participants, a diverse group ranging from twenty-two to sixty-seven years old, about their anticipated holiday hiccups. "I'm not looking forward to the questions," a young woman piped up: "'Do you have a boyfriend? Are you working yet?'" The other faces on the screen began nodding in unison like a sea of pixelated bobbleheads. "Exactly," a man chimed in. "How am I supposed to tell my Great Aunt Mary that I've spent the past three months on leave from work to attend day treatment for severe OCD? She just wants to know why I'm still living with my parents." Quickly, my plan to talk about targeted response prevention during the holidays evaporated as people shared their stresses about family interactions. Instead, we concentrated on navigating the intricacies of familial relationships while managing (and sometimes hiding) OCD.

Let's be real: families can be stressful with or without mental health concerns. A group of people bound together by shared circumstances (and often shared genes) can be our best allies *and* our harshest critics. They know just how to comfort us *and* how to find the precise location of our last nerve so that they can poke it. My brother can provoke me with just a tiny smirk, unleashing the petulant seven-year-old within. When you marry into other families, there's a whole new set of quirks and customs to unpack. With all our family members, similar questions arise. Who can you trust with information about your mental health? How can you maintain authentic connections without being pulled into the well-worn grooves of old family dynamics? In this chapter, we'll discuss how OCD affects families, identifying and challenging familial stories about OCD, managing disclosure with family, and enlisting family members as allies in your treatment, and we will also talk about how OCD affects relationships with pets.

How OCD Affects the Whole Family

It used to be de rigueur for therapists to blame anything and everything on our clients' parents. There are still plenty of clinicians who emphasize the impact of our so-called families of origin (FOO) on current behavior and symptoms. And although that's an important piece of the picture, our families are but one tiny piece of a mosaic of genetic, environmental, physiological, cultural, and social influences that contribute to our behavior. It would be downright FOO-lish to reduce our complex behavior to mere passive responses to our families. However, it's true that our relationships with family members can motivate or subdue our desires to kick OCD out of the driver's seat. Supportive families hold us gently as we tackle the hard work of therapy and provide soft places to land when things get difficult. Unsupportive families, on the other hand, may contribute to our stress, shame, and anxiety. Therefore, determining how best to cultivate familial relationships that encourage constructive growth (or at least don't undermine it) is a worthwhile endeavor.

Chapter 2 talked about how some of the things that feel the most like caretaking from others—accommodating symptoms, such as "rescuing" you from triggers—can actually perpetuate OCD symptoms. Womp, womp. Of course, having loved ones dismiss, criticize, or trivialize your concerns is also unhelpful—although you probably didn't need a book to tell you that! While most of the research on family responses to OCD has been done with children with OCD, these patterns are also true for adults (Albert, Baffa, and Maina 2017). If your family consistently bends over backwards to make sure that you don't feel any distress, you may never learn how resilient you can be. At its extreme, such family accommodation can reduce your motivation for change and keep you stuck in the OCD cycle. However, if your family members don't change their behavior at all to meet you where you are with symptoms, you'll feel demoralized and misunderstood. It's a delicate balance, and most families struggle to get it right.

While family members' responses to you can impact your OCD, your OCD impacts family members as well. Your family cares about you, and it makes sense that they would feel stressed when you do. They may blame themselves or experience helplessness about your symptoms or have difficulty taking time to engage in self-care and independent activities. I once watched a respected colleague give a talk to parents of young adults with OCD who were receiving intensive treatment. She asked the audience if any of them had read a book in the last week. Over half of the hands shot up. "A book not about OCD or mental health," she clarified, and many of the hands fell. She encouraged them to consider doing something simple, like carving out an hour a week to just read for pleasure, and you'd have thought that she'd asked them to jump off a cliff. They had forgotten how to take care of themselves while they were busy caring for their children. But doing so wasn't helping anyone—neither their loved ones with OCD nor themselves. It's a "put your oxygen mask on first before helping others" situation. Family members may also confuse the idea of protecting your privacy as someone with OCD with cutting themselves off from their own support, effectively "hiding" from the world. This reinforces the very stigma that family members are trying to protect against. When I work with families who are open about OCD, I see much more of a team approach to symptom reduction, integrating support from both family and community.

Including family members in the treatment of adult children can improve outcomes too. In a recent review of research in this area, family-inclusive treatment for adult OCD was found to improve symptoms of OCD, depression, and anxiety while reducing OCD's impact on other areas of life such as work and socializing. Additionally, both the people with OCD and their family members reported better relationships, marked by less accommodation and conflict (Stewart, Sumantry, and Malivoire 2020).

Of course, you may not have a family that's willing to come to therapy sessions, or you may not feel that your family would support you in this way. My heart goes out to you, and please know that this says nothing about your worth or ability to have a fulfilling life with OCD. If you fall into this category, later sections in this chapter on boundary setting may be particularly helpful.

Unpacking Family Stories About OCD

Because OCD runs in families, you may not be the only one among your relatives with symptoms. Sometimes OCD is so woven into family trees that it's like a vine snaking through the branches and blending in with the bark beneath. "We're a family of apologizers," some clients will proclaim. Or in other cases, "Everyone goes to the doctor at the drop of a hat!" Having others with lived experience in your family can be a salve for feelings of isolation or shame. It can also set the tone for how therapy is pursued (or if it is at all). Even if there are multiple relatives with OCD, the ways that they've dealt with their symptoms might vary based on generational differences, symptom severity, specific themes, or access to therapy.

While some families have a keen eye for recognizing and addressing OC-normal symptoms, others have a culture of burying any evidence of OCD to conform to social norms. Some of the most painful stories I hear are about relatives with severe symptoms who never received proper diagnosis or treatment and who became the black sheep of the family. These stories often start out like, "Well, no one really talks about Grandpa Larry," and center on a relative with severe OCD whose symptoms prevented them from living a typical life. Often the family members of those who were cast aside have a pessimistic view of how OCD limits the fullness of life.

Or maybe you are the only one in your family with OCD—or at least the only one you know of. In the absence of a set family narrative about OCD, you may still be subject to other stories about mental health more generally. If therapy and mental wellness are embraced as part of the greater goal of health, your family may provide supportive encouragement, curiosity, and an exploration of interventions. On the other hand, if mental illness is seen as a sign of weakness or isn't recognized as valid, you may feel compelled to hide your symptoms. Adopted people with OCD often feel the double sting of loneliness if others in their family are unfamiliar with OCD. This can feel like more evidence of otherness when compared to the rest of the family.

All this is to say that every family has a story about what OCD or mental illness is, how it affects people, and how it should be approached. These stories affect how we all understand and communicate about mental health topics. Sometimes identifying your family narratives about OCD can help you with disclosing to others in the family and anticipating the supports or roadblocks you may encounter when advocating for yourself. Doing this exercise may also compel you to question your own narratives about OCD and help you to rewrite your own OCD story with abundant compassion and hope.

Use the "Challenging Your Family Narrative About OCD" worksheet available at http://www.newharbinger.com/50584 to complete these prompts:

1. My family believes that mental illness is…

2. When it comes to mental health, my family…

3. In my family, OCD…

4.   In my family, therapy is…

5.   In my family, medication for mental health is…

These sentence stems are deliberately open-ended, so try not to worry about completing them "correctly," which I know can be hard with OCD! The point is to see what comes up for you when you reflect on your family's stance toward mental illness and OCD. You can do this activity for your immediate family members, extended family, family by marriage, or anyone else who's important to you.

After completing these prompts, you can use them to write out your family's narrative or narratives (there is likely more than one!). Here's what one person wrote:

> *My family believes that mental illness is overdiagnosed and used as a way for people to get sympathy and special treatment. Maintaining good mental health is seen as an individual responsibility rather than as something for which people might seek help. This is especially true for men in the family. While women are "allowed" to cry or have anxiety, men are ridiculed for showing any emotions. On the other hand, men are "allowed" to drink excessively without judgment, while women are condemned for the same behavior. Going to therapy is seen as a failure, and taking medication means that you're too weak to pull yourself up by the bootstraps and take care of your own needs. We all learned to keep it secret if we were having any struggles or going to therapy. OCD was never discussed, even though it seems to run in the family. Family members who struggle with compulsions were ridiculed for their behavior.*

Whoa! You can see how this kind of narrative would influence the writer's thoughts about OCD and about sharing this experience with others. If there are parts of your own family narrative that you would like to challenge, you can underline them in your story and come up with alternative beliefs. For example, in the narrative above, this person selected the following sentence to challenge: "Maintaining good mental health is seen as an individual responsibility rather than as something for which people might seek help." Their alternative thought was: *It's responsible and self-compassionate to seek help with mental health challenges.* These new thoughts and beliefs can help you treat yourself with kindness and advocate for your needs.

Disclosure in Family Relationships

Figuring out the who, what, when, where, why, and how of sharing your OCD with family, as with other people, is often a complicated personal decision. Certain family may be natural choices for disclosure due to their caring natures or their own histories of anxiety/OCD. Others may be off-limits, if they haven't earned your trust or shown sensitive behavior. And if you do disclose, remember that you have lots of options! You can talk about having anxiety, mention your OCD diagnosis specifically, delve into the details of your content, or any combination thereof. You can use many methods, enlisting books or videos for help or bringing multiple people together to save time. Telling others about OCD is an exposure unto itself, as your information, once dropped neatly into the lap of your family member, can be digested in any number of ways. It may be integrated thoughtfully into their understanding of you and lead to lasting change in your relationship. Or it may be rejected, invalidated, or even used against you in anger. In short, choosing to disclose is kind of a paradise for OCD to spin out in a frenzy of rumination.

Anxiety often compels us to catastrophize when we try something new—to think about the worst possible outcomes of any given change—but it rarely has us consider the positives that may come from doing something new or the negatives of staying the same. Using a decisional balance grid can help you explore all the positives and negatives in making this kind of decision (Miller and Rose 2015).

Decisional Balance Grid: *Guiding Your Disclosure*

Draw a grid in your journal or on a piece of paper labeled like the one depicted here. Then list the pros and cons of no disclosure versus disclosure to family members.

	Pros	Cons
No Disclosure		
Disclosure		

Use this exercise to explore whether to tell family members about your OCD, if you've been struggling with the decision.

Depending on a variety of circumstances, including your family narratives about OCD, making this decision can be more or less complicated.

Jada's Story

Jada, a thirty-three-year-old woman, had experienced OCD symptoms from a young age but didn't receive a formal diagnosis until she was in her early thirties. Her family had always characterized her as anxious and perfectionistic, but in the absence of any overt cleaning or repeating, they never considered that it could be OCD. Instead, Jada experienced primarily just right and checking behaviors, which were most pronounced when she did transitional tasks like leaving the house, exiting her car, or winding down to go to sleep. But to others in her life, Jada just looked like someone with poor time management. In fact, her mother jokingly added Jada's "dawdle time" to the family's schedule any time they had to leave the house. This symptom accommodation was ultimately harmful to Jada, as it didn't give her a chance to challenge her symptoms. But it helped her family to embrace what they saw as quirks of her personality. Jada never felt ashamed of her symptoms, but she also never learned to alter her patterns.

Jada also attributed her family's failure to recognize her OCD in childhood to cultural factors. She told me that as a Black woman, she had never seen depictions of OCD that included people of color and didn't know of any therapy resources in her community. And while she and her family were sensitive to mental health concerns, they believed in remedying emotional and behavioral issues within the home rather than in a therapist's office.

Limited representation, reduced access to care, and mistrust of behavioral health providers are common for Black Americans with OCD (Williams, Debreaux, and Jahn 2016). Some of these concerns showed up in Jada's decisional balance grid when exploring whether to disclose her OCD to her family:

	Pros	Cons
No Change	Parents aren't as worried. Don't draw attention to myself. Don't have to defend going to therapy.	Must continue making up excuses for my behavior. Continue feeling inauthentic with family.

Disclose	Parents understand why I take so long to get ready.	Parents could invalidate me.
	May find out that others in the family can relate.	May be treated differently by family.
	May feel better understood.	Could lead to conflict about missed diagnosis in childhood.
	No longer must hide OCD behaviors.	Could lead to conflict about therapy.
	Can educate family about OCD.	

You may notice when completing your grid that many of your pros and cons are hypothetical, especially when it comes to predicting how others will react or their receptivity to learning about OCD. What you can control, however, is your own action. In Jada's case, this meant controlling whether to continue to hide or make excuses for her slower behavior. Areas of uncertainty are typical when deciding about disclosure, so don't expect that your answer will emerge from the decisional grid with the certainty that your OCD probably wants.

Jada did end up telling her parents about her OCD diagnosis. Her mother was understanding and receptive to her disclosure, expressing a desire to learn as much as possible to support her, but her father was somewhat dismissive, saying that "Everyone has struggles" and that labeling herself was harmful. Her mother reflected that Jada's paternal aunt had showed similar symptoms throughout her life as well as excessive reassurance seeking and health anxiety, and that her father's reluctance to accept Jada's diagnosis might be tied to difficulty accepting that his sister had a mental health concern that went undiagnosed and untreated. Put another way, his OCD narrative was influenced by this experience and made his acceptance of Jada's OCD more difficult. Thankfully, with educational resources and time, he eventually committed to being an ally in her treatment.

Managing Guilt After Disclosure

Sometimes with disclosure and talking about OCD with family, feelings of guilt can arise for both you and your family members. For you, it may feel like an obligation to apologize for having a mental health condition or for spending time and resources on treatment. For them, it may look like seeking assurance that they didn't cause your OCD or expressing regret for not having gotten you help sooner. Here are a couple of tips to keep guilt from being the loudest voice in the room.

First, remember that your OCD isn't your fault. No one would choose the pain that you've felt in trying to manage the strong emotions, unpredictable urges, and repetitive behaviors you've endured. I know that just saying that doesn't change the feeling. Guilt can be so convincing in part because of something that we call *emotional reasoning,* which is the tendency for us to believe that something is true because it feels that way. With OCD, your experience of guilt may appear to be proof enough that you've transgressed or messed up. But just as you would never tell a loved one that they caused their mental illness, turn some of that compassion on yourself. You can recognize that having OCD is painful without telling a story of culpability to make sense of the feelings.

Family members may express guilt too and may ask for you to assuage their guilt. It's not their fault that you have OCD either, but it's also not your responsibility to take care of them in this case. In fact, you may have some negative feelings about the way that your family reacted to your symptoms, and that's perfectly valid! You may even feel disappointment or anger that they never helped you access care or that they pooh-poohed your symptoms as fussiness. Having negative feelings is valid even if your family members were unaware of OCD as a possibility or if they did the best that they could with the resources that they had. This stuff's tricky, and the last thing that I would want anyone with OCD to have to do is to soothe others while stifling their own suffering. How then do we make room for the onslaught of conflicting emotions that may arise?

You can use some of the skills we've touched upon in earlier chapters to help stay present. Mindful self-compassion is one such skill that can help here. You can recognize the suffering that both you and your loved ones may hold and just allow it to exist without the meaning-making that we are so quick to do. You can recognize that these feelings are ones that have been experienced by others who've suffered and thus bring an open sense of curiosity to the conversation. In the spirit of mindfulness and staying in the present moment, you can also highlight to family members how even if they didn't know how to respond to your symptoms in the past, they can use this information to do better now. This "know better, do better" mentality doesn't erase any of the pain of the past, but it does set an expectation for family members that the best way to help you out is to remain in the here and now.

Tools for Fostering Better Family Relationships

Family relationships can run the gamut from helpful to harmful, with some relatives acting as our biggest allies and others better left without access to our inner worlds. If you choose to disclose to others, you may benefit from providing them with education about OCD and how they can support you. If you choose not to disclose or you feel that your loved ones' criticism or misunderstanding gets in the way of your relationship, you can practice assertive communication and boundary setting.

Educating Your Family About OCD

In your thirst for information about OCD, this book may be one in a series of books, articles, social media accounts, and websites you've perused, looking for answers to normalize your seemingly unusual experience. Well, now it's time for the student to become the teacher, as you pass along your wisdom to your family. After disclosure, your relatives may have questions about OCD, and you'll likely be the one to educate them. This can feel exciting. At the same time, you may find OCD difficult to explain to others. It can feel hard enough to understand OCD when you have it, let alone if you're looking at it from the outside. What's more, you may have to field questions about your judgment, confront stigma head-on, or feel like you must justify your OCD to others.

Over the past fifteen years, I've watched scores of clients grapple with this process. Sometimes we do joint family education sessions, and sometimes my clients opt to go it alone, armed with books and articles to help their family members. As a witness to this process, my clients have taught me some of the most important lessons to include in your OCD 101 crash course. While this is by no means a complete list, it contains elements designed to help reduce friction and misunderstanding in the family.

OCD doesn't follow or respond to logic. Well-meaning family members may attempt to challenge your fears or doubts with facts or even argue with your symptoms. And as you know, OCD has a way of arguing back. So, when others point out the logical fallacies in your symptoms, they run the risk of provoking not only a cascade of *yeah I know, but what-ifs* from your OCD but also feelings of incompetence or shame. Consider letting family members know that you're aware of the ways in which OCD departs from logic and that this departure adds to the frustration you feel about your symptoms.

OCD symptoms look different for everyone. There's a wealth of information available about OCD and its many forms. However, family members may read one account of what it's like to have symptoms and attempt to extrapolate your experience from this. Letting family members know that you want them to listen to your personal experience rather than make assumptions based on other experiences (including, potentially, their own!) is a great way to cut off miscommunication at the pass.

OCD treatment is gradual and progressive. Much of the information available for family members centers on the reduction of accommodation, and for good reason. Reducing unhelpful accommodation is one of the most powerful tools that loved ones can use to help you fight your symptoms. But there's nuance in the approach to reducing accommodation that may be lost on family. They may read about compulsive reassurance seeking and immediately stop providing it altogether, which is both scary and unhelpful. This ham-fisted approach can strain relationships and increase symptoms. Family members will benefit from learning that some flexibility in their behavior around your symptoms may be necessary as you embark on your treatment journey. They may also need to be reminded that everyone's timeline is different, and that sometimes what seems to be a small step to them is a giant leap for you.

People with OCD can't just stop. Just like you can realize that an obsession is illogical but still feel an intense emotional response to it, it's hard to stop doing compulsions even when you know they're unhelpful. It's important to explain to family that this isn't because of low motivation or weak will; the reasons for it can be found at the neurological level. That is, people with OCD tend to perform less well than those without OCD on *inhibitory control tasks,* tasks that require you to perform actions repeatedly and then stop doing them based on certain cues.

That last bit was clear as mud, right? An example of an *inhibitory control task* from the real world would be the children's game Simon Says. In this game, you're supposed to do everything that the leader says to do—usually simple physical gestures—when the leader says "Simon says" and gives a command. If the leader doesn't say "Simon says" before giving a command, you're supposed to remain still. So if the leader says, "Simon says, clap your hands," and you clap your hands, and then the leader says "Stomp your feet," and you stomp your feet, you're out of the game. You're also showing limited inhibitory control. People with inhibitory control difficulties have more trouble stopping a behavior that they're used to completing, like when it feels hard to stop engaging in a compulsion loop. Compared to people without mental health conditions, the brains of people with OCD show increased activation in certain areas and decreased activity in others when they complete these kinds of tasks (Norman et al. 2019). So, unless your family members can magically alter your brain with their "Stop that!" commands, they can at least be patient as you work to change your neural patterns.

Setting Boundaries with Family Members

Regardless of whether and to what extent you choose to disclose to your family, it's important that you feel empowered to advocate for yourself with relatives. This can be especially tricky with older relatives, as you may have had years of experience being deferential toward them. Recall from chapter 7 that assertive communication can be a powerful tool in ensuring that your needs are met. It can also be helpful in the process of setting boundaries with family. Boundaries are guidelines that help us define our separation from others, emotionally and physically, so that we can feel comfortable, safe, and respected. For example, you can set boundaries in terms of your time, the topics you're willing to discuss, or the activities you'll willing to engage in.

With family, setting boundaries around time spent together is a common way to mitigate conflict. During the holidays, for example, you may let your family know that you can spend three out of five evenings with them while you're in town, as you will be spending time with friends on the other evenings. You can also let your family know if there are certain topics that are off-limits, such as talking about your weight or marital status. Remember that setting a boundary doesn't mean that your family will accept it, but it does outline what you are and aren't willing to tolerate. Be careful not to confuse boundaries with rationales for avoiding triggers, however. For example, if you know that your dad's side of the family smokes and your OCD has concerns about contamination from second-hand smoke, it will only fuel your OCD to completely disengage from that side of the family. It would, however, be appropriate to ask your relatives not to smoke in your home and to challenge yourself to let your values rather than your symptoms lead the way.

Having OCD When You Have Pets

The final topic of this chapter has to do with our so-called fur babies, or pet family members. Like many people, you may think of your pets as another member of the family, and research shows that it might be better for your health to do so. In one study, participants who viewed their pets as family members derived more social support from their pets and experienced greater well-being. This is in line with other research that shows people who consider Fluffy "family" show higher levels of physical and mental health compared with those who don't (McConnell, Paige Lloyd, and Humphrey 2019). But if you have a pet, you probably already know this. Companion animals can not only provide emotional support but add structure and rhythm to your life. Taking care of a pet allows you to step outside of yourself to provide for someone else. And given everything we know about OCD's propensity to attack whatever we most value, you may not be surprised to hear that pets are also a frequent target for obsessions and compulsions.

While the ways that OCD can target pets are as varied as other OC-normal thoughts, a few themes tend to rise to the top. Pets are often seen as contaminants or as sources of the spread of contamination. That is, touching your pet's fur, feathers, or scales may provoke urges to wash your hands, and smelling their breath may provoke an urge to expel air forcefully. Their bodily waste may also be seen as contamination. Additionally, animals move around, so you may worry about them spreading other forms of contamination, sort of like cross-pollinators for whatever OCD says is dirty. Furthermore, given their vulnerable nature, pets can be a natural target for harm and responsibility themes too. Double-checking to make sure that crates are latched or enclosures are secured, inspecting pets for signs of bodily harm, and avoiding doing certain actions (such as using low-risk cleaners) around pets are all compulsions designed to trick you into the illusion of preventing harm to your companion. Unwanted sexual thoughts can occur as well (and the pictures I have of my dog's undercarriage on my phone for exposure purposes are a testament to this!). Remember, if it's weird, scary, taboo, or gross, it's fair game for OCD. And because I've specifically gotten this question multiple times while writing this book, yes, you can have ROCD with your pet. Wondering if you love them enough or if they'll abandon you can all be part of the way that OCD attacks the things we cherish.

As with any other relationship, it's important to reduce and eventually eliminate compulsions surrounding animal companions. Doing so can help you make sure that your behavior with your pet is based on your love for them rather than dictated by fear or avoidance. So take a step back to think about the kinds of things that really deepen your relationship with your pet. If you have an aversion to hair along with a Persian cat who considers brushing the highest form of pampering, your values may lead you straight into a loving moment that also provokes your OCD. While your pet can't verbalize how much they appreciate it, you can feel better knowing that your bond is rooted in something other than your fears or uncertainty.

Family Matters

Each family makes up its own world with unwritten rules, social customs, and beliefs about mental health. Defining your own beliefs about your OCD can help you decide about disclosing to family and how you advocate for support. I hope that the activities in this chapter have been helpful in improving your relationships with family. The next chapter will move on to managing OCD when you have children, as we talk about the wonderful and terrifying world of parenting with OCD.

CHAPTER 9

Managing OCD While Managing Kids
Parenting with OCD

Children are a blessing. But from their earliest moments, it turns out, they're also tiny, messy, and unpredictable exposure machines. Many of the things that your OCD craves—certainty, security, comfort, and control—will be tossed aside like carrots by a toddler once you become the caretaker of a little one. Do you have a routine down pat? Not anymore. A clear vision of the next five years of your life? Maybe the next five minutes if you're lucky! Are you experiencing one of the greatest and most profound loves that you can possibly feel? Sure, but that also means that you have more to lose should something bad happen to your kids. Raising children may be the ultimate cage match between valued actions and fear-based avoidance. Of all my clients' fears, their worry about their fitness to raise children is one of the most heartbreaking. You may not make any room for family in your dreams for the future, because you've been convinced that you can't have one. It's my goal in this chapter to challenge that notion outright and provide skills and tools to mitigate the impact of your OCD on your family planning or parenting.

Parents with OCD can be fantastic caretakers who cultivate rich attachments with their children. Many of my clients count family as a strong value, and some cite this as their primary motivation for reducing their own symptoms. These parents are everything that parents without

OCD are but with the added special superpower that comes from tussling with a fierce inner opponent. If you're a parent with OCD, you're both capable and worthy of having a fulfilling relationship with your children. This is true regardless of how much your OCD content has glommed onto your kids. Remember that OCD's content tends to latch onto areas that are important to you, taking advantage of your values to "hit you where it hurts." Otherwise, your intrusive thoughts would feel less jarring and more like odd brain quirks, and your compulsions would feel less like obligations and more like choices.

OCD in Parents

Children being incorporated into OCD themes can occur across symptom subtypes, sometimes in the most painful of ways. With responsibility themes, this can look like excessive checking behaviors and rigid guidelines because OCD has focused on the possibility that your child will be physically or emotionally harmed. With harm OCD, it can include worries about harming your children yourself, and these intrusions may be so disturbing that you end up withdrawing from your kids "for their safety." Similarly, pedophilia-themed OCD may result in the avoidance of bathing your child or changing diapers due to worries about engaging in sexual abuse either accidentally or during a temporary loss of control. Contamination concerns can conjure worries about your child bringing in unwanted germs or contaminants into the home, concerns about their health, and excessive cleaning protocols foisted on children. Just right concerns may result in parent–child conflict, as (not surprisingly) kids' natural inclinations usually fall outside of what OCD considers "just right."

I could go on. For every theme of OCD, there are ways that it can infiltrate the parent–child relationship or enlist kids in the OCD cycle. Unfortunately, many parents with taboo thoughts choose not to disclose their worries to providers for fear that they'll be labeled as a threat or that their children will be removed from them. This heaps on additional stress, as parents are left to deal with thoughts that tap into the deepest well of their grief while going it alone. Furthermore, symptoms can affect children indirectly. Appeasing OCD may reduce your ability to be present with your child physically and emotionally.

Ryan's Story

Ryan, a forty-one-year-old father of three, had experienced mild symptoms of OCD as a child but found that they skyrocketed after the birth of his daughter twelve years ago. Although he attributed this to the increased stress of having an infant in the home, his symptoms never directly focused on her or the other children. His primary fear was of contracting oral or genital herpes. Ryan expressed embarrassment about this theme, reassuring himself aloud that he hadn't engaged in any behaviors that would expose him to the virus. His pain was greatest, however, when he discussed a recent family vacation.

"My wife loaded up the kids and drove the eight hours to the coast," he explained. He, on the other hand, left the following morning by plane. "I knew it was irrational, even stupid," he grimaced, "but I couldn't bear the thought of stopping at a gas station restroom and touching anything there. My OCD made it so that I missed out on hours of time with my family. And I put all the work of traveling on my wife." Shortly thereafter, he began treatment using an ERP and ACT framework. Exposures centered on reclaiming avoided places, interacting with "contaminated" people, reading firsthand accounts about herpes, and placing himself in what his OCD perceived to be high-risk situations. Response prevention included reducing washing behaviors and eliminating a whole host of mental rituals that had provided the illusion of safety.

As he got a handle on his fears, Ryan appreciated being able to engage with the world in a less restrained way, and even more so, he appreciated how he was able to free up time to reconnect with his children. He had more time to attend dance recitals, help with homework, and read bedtime stories as his compulsions shrank. But it was only when his seven-year-old daughter remarked, "Daddy, you're smiling a lot now," that he realized how much his symptoms had impacted the whole family.

You have a choice in those moments when your symptoms make demands of your time or attention. Again, the choice is ultimately between receiving short-term relief and moving toward a life dictated by you and not by your OCD, and starting with a clear set of values for that life can be an empowering step. You can explore your values in parenting, just as you explored your values in friendship in chapter 4 and in romantic relationships in chapter 5.

Parenting Road Map: *Exploring Your Values*

Retrieve your list of values from chapter 4, and identify which of these values are most important to convey to your children through your parenting. As a challenge, avoid words like "safety" or "order" that are easily blown out of proportion by your OCD. Give yourself a moment to really think about which values are most important, and see where your heart leads you. This is your family, and these are your unique values. If you're having difficulty finding the right words, it may be helpful to ask yourself, *How do I want my little person to engage with the world?* Perhaps adventure or compassion feel important. Or you may ask, *Where do I want my child to invest their energy?* Faith or industry may rise to the top. Or, *What kind of relationships do I want to have with my kids?* Honesty? Fun?

I grew up next door to a family of five in which the parents were visual artists, and I frequently spent my days as a child playing at their house and experimenting with art supplies. As artists, the parents valued the skill of being mindful of your surroundings and taking time to notice things. I found myself contributing to dinner conversations with descriptions of the gnarled oak tree I'd seen on the edge of the park or the way that their dog's fur made a zigzag across her back. "How observant of you!" the dad would tell me. I was both cultivating my skills of observation and connecting with these adults in a meaningful way. My own family had other values, such as independence and humor, but my parents weren't particularly "stop and smell the roses" types. I attribute my earliest experiences of mindfulness to these dinners with our neighbors. Interactions like these can be significant in shaping a child's exploration of different values.

The identification of your parenting values is an integral part of enacting behavioral change. After getting in touch with these *whys*, you can then take on the difficult work of *what* you will change, using the "Parenting Exposure Hierarchy" available at http://www.newharbinger. com/50584. Choose three to five values that you'd most like to convey to your children and write them down at the top of the worksheet. In the first column, list those values that you want to express but currently avoid.

Now think about how your OCD has limited your ability to convey these values to your child either directly (by having kids engage in certain behaviors or avoid certain situations) or indirectly (by modeling behaviors to the contrary). Use this information to generate a few exposures that you can engage in to demonstrate values-based parenting while challenging OCD. It may be helpful to ask yourself, *What would I do differently to convey this value if I weren't limited by OCD?* After writing down these exposures, rate each one on a scale of 1 to 10 to indicate your willingness to try them, where 1 indicates that you are completely unwilling to try this exposure now and 10 means that you're willing to jump in as soon as possible. Here are a couple of examples.

Value	Parenting Exposure	Willingness

| Friendship | I'll allow my daughter to climb on the jungle gym with her friends at the park. | 4 |
| Independence | I won't require my teen to text me every hour when he goes out. | 8 |

You may use additional worksheets to come up with more exposure items. Again, focusing on your values is a wonderful way to harness your motivation toward challenging OCD's rules. Over time, you can advance up the hierarchy, starting with those exposures that you're most willing to do and working your way up to the most challenging ones.

Inflated Responsibility and Parenting

As a child, I had an outsized amount of compassion for earthworms. After a summer downpour, I would tiptoe around the sidewalk in front of my house, "rescuing" the worms that had wriggled their way out of the mud and onto the path of oncoming foot traffic. I'd pick up the worms gingerly and return them to the mud one by one, taking care not to leave anyone out. This behavior reflected my belief that any worm on the concrete was a worm in distress and that it was my personal responsibility to protect them from harm. With inflated responsibility, you have the belief that it's necessary not only to refrain from harming others but also to prevent harm whenever possible. It's like being a worm rescuer all grown up. People with OCD tend to score higher on levels of inflated responsibility than people without the disorder (Gwilliam, Wells, and Cartwright-Hatton 2004).

When you add children to your family through childbirth, adoption, or other means, your level of responsibility objectively increases. This increase, when combined with a tendency to hold yourself to high standards of harm prevention, creates fertile ground for OCD symptoms to flourish. Many people with OCD experience an exacerbation in symptoms after adding a child to the family (Buchholz, Hellberg, and

Abramowitz 2020). This change occurs in partners and adoptive parents as well as in people who have just given birth, which suggests that increased symptoms are not solely a by-product of hormonal turmoil. The addition of caretaking a vulnerable individual can be a catalyst for increased symptoms. Throw lack of sleep and disruptions in routine into the mix, and you're off to the races!

So, you have a brain that's telling you about the importance of preventing harm and a baby whose instincts are to explore the world through putting things in an electrical outlet or by licking that weird spot on the floor. It may not feel...ideal. But here's the annoying part of the chapter where the author, an OCD therapist, tells you that raising children provides a wonderful opportunity to practice mindfully being in the presence of distressing emotions, accepting uncertainty, and choosing not to respond to compulsive urges. And there are related benefits for kids if you're able to quell the influence of inflated responsibility. Parents who engage in reasonable levels of autonomy-granting (letting kids make their own decisions) raise kids with lower levels of anxiety (McLeod, Wood, and Weisz 2007).

Moving Toward Helpful and Responsible

If you're struggling with figuring out the cutoff between helpful, responsible parenting and unhelpful, hyperresponsible parenting, here are a few strategies to clarify the difference:

Gather evidence from others you respect. It's important that this strategy be focused on speaking with credible sources and that you limit your time on it, as researching and reassurance seeking are common compulsive behaviors. With a co-parent or co-parents, you can explore ideas about what's necessary to provide safety and security. Make sure that you listen without interrupting and without generating hypothetical situations from which to argue your opposition. Ban the word "but" from this conversation. You can also ask for input from your child's pediatrician, other family members whose opinions you respect, faith leaders, community members, or friends whose values are like yours. For example, you may ask about things like the frequency of checking on your sleeping kids, how often they recommend touching base with teachers, cleaning practices in the home, or whether it's reasonable to have a GPS device implanted directly into the body of a rebellious teenager! The purpose isn't to come up with a definitive list of noncompulsive parenting practices, and you'll still have to make the final determination of what works for your family. But this process may help you stop to evaluate whether the practices that you deem responsible are excessively restrictive.

Compare the cons of your current parenting with the pros of changing it. Remember that the obsessive-compulsive brain is excellent at engaging in risk management. The brain can default to "if it's safer, it's better," which is a slippery and never-ending slope of restrictions and precautions. It's time to let your brain explore the other side of the decision tree. For example, what's lost by continuing with your current safety measures and parenting practices? Perhaps your children are missing out on important social interactions or experiences that will help them to feel more independent. Perhaps they're missing out on seeing a parent's smile (as in Ryan's story above). And how might changing the current practices help both you and your child feel more confident over time? If it helps to do so, sit down with a co-parent or another loved one to explore these questions.

Remember that thoughts are different from actions. When you contemplate the feared outcomes of changing your behaviors, you may have thoughts or images that feel almost too scary to say aloud. This is OC-normal and shows how important your children really are to you (or else the thoughts wouldn't feel so abhorrent). However, if you are plagued by thoughts of harming your child and therefore avoid using knives to cook while your child is around, you're confusing the thought of harm with acting on it. This is an example of thought–action fusion, which can make thoughts and actions feel equivalent. Remind yourself that, while it's understandable to have a strong reaction to a vivid thought, what's going on in your head is still in your head. As uncomfortable as such thoughts and emotions are, you'll survive having them. Restrictive or ritualistic behaviors, on the other hand, can have real and immediate impacts on kids.

Talk to your children. Be curious about your kids' experience of your rules and safety protocols. This may not be fruitful with very young children (who may want to abolish bedtimes and petition that all surfaces in the home be used primarily for coloring), but it can be quite eye-opening to have this conversation with older children. They may help to elucidate some of the downsides for children associated with your inflated responsibility, such as playtime lost to frequently checking in with parents, frustration about having to eat only "clean" foods, or embarrassment about handwashing protocols when friends visit the home. Listen with compassion for not only them but also yourself. You're not engaging in any of these behaviors to deliberately harm your children—quite the opposite! Your brain has told you that doing this will be safer. By opening space for your children to tell you how your symptoms are impacting them, you can start to collaborate and build a plan to reduce these impacts.

Letting Go of Perfect

With experience, most parents usually relax their standards, as they learn via natural exposure that babies are resilient. One of the many gifts of the internet is the wellspring of content about parents raising their first child versus later ones. I've seen memes with captions like this: "First child: swaddled head-to-toe in new clothing, sucking on an ergonomic pacifier. Second child: wearing hand-me-downs, chewing on a broken teething ring. Third child: sporting a stained onesie, sucking on one of the dog's toys." It's helpful for new parents to recognize that momentary inattentiveness or poor decision making is unlikely to irrevocably harm their children. The truth is, there's no such thing as a perfect parent and standards are bound to change over time.

Even so, there's still a lot of pressure as a parent to be perfect, and having OCD can make the perfectionistic voice much louder. This voice can say all kinds of alarming things. A child playing outside in the snow suddenly becomes a recipe for frostbite and limb loss. The inner voice crows, *You'd better research all the coats and gloves available and buy the warmest coat even if it's a few decades behind style-wise. And when your child comes home embarrassed because everyone else is wearing the latest style, you'd better find another coat so that you don't see them being bullied into severe depression and one day committing a mass shooting.* And then maybe you move on to worrying about what other parents will say about your propensity to continue buying new coats. Are they going to think that your child is spoiled? That's the way that perfectionism works: it's a moving target that demands more and more of your time while providing less and less certainty and security. Additionally, being perfect is an abstract concept that is unachievable in the real world. There will always be something better out there. And even as you approach your ideal parenting behavior, the perfectionistic brain always focuses on the discrepancy between where you are now and what perfection would look like, even if that gap is narrow.

Usually, perfectionism is bolstered by the stories we tell ourselves about effort and standards. You may believe that strict adherence to perfectionistic standards will keep your children safe or your mental health stable. This next exercise will help you find alternatives for perfectionistic thinking.

Perfectionistic Thinking: *Finding Alternatives*

Read this list of perfectionistic thoughts, and if any resonate with you, write them in your journal. Share these thoughts with loved ones and see if they have alternative perspectives.

If I don't do things perfectly...

...Physical harm will befall my child.

...My child will feel unloved.

...I'll become more and more lax until I'm neglectful.

...My family or community will judge me.

...My child will be judged or ostracized.

...I'll completely lose control.

...I'll be too distressed to recover.

Now read this list of alternative thoughts, and see if any appeal to you as a way to reframe your own thinking.

By allowing myself to parent imperfectly...

...I'm giving my child opportunities to figure things out on their own.

...I'm freeing up my brain to concentrate on developing the connections I desire with my child.

...I'm fostering my child's resilience.

...I'm developing flexibility.

...I'm practicing accepting myself as only human.

...I'm modeling healthy standards for my child.

...I'm prioritizing my mental health over my OCD's rules.

Write down the alternative thoughts that most appeal to you in your journal, or put them on sticky notes around your bedroom or as the screensaver on your phone. Be creative! Then, when your old beliefs rear up, you can remind yourself to embrace being human instead of striving for perfection.

All parents, including the most empathic, thoughtful, and patient ones, parent imperfectly. Despite this, your OCD may tell you that you must be the one exception to the rule. If your anxiety demands flawlessness from you, remember that while you can't be perfect, you can choose to be self-compassionate and real. This will help both you and your child in the long run.

Maintaining Your Role as a Parent

Like all important relationships, the parent–child relationship thrives when it's grounded in a sense of mutual respect. However, parents have the additional task of providing for children their very first sense of attachment to others and a safe base from which they can explore the world. No pressure! Thankfully, we have a wealth of data on what kinds of parenting support healthy child outcomes. Parents who show high levels of responsiveness and warmth combined with high expectations of their kids have children who fare better on several different fronts, including emotion regulation, academic functioning, and social skills, and they are less likely to have behavioral issues or internalizing disorders (like depression and anxiety). This style of parenting, called authoritative parenting, is beneficial across various cultures worldwide (Pinquart and Kauser 2018). Put simply, to flourish, kids need both warmth and encouragement and high expectations of their conduct. The former may look like spending quality time with your children and validating their emotional experiences, while the latter may look like enforcing age-appropriate demands and setting clear parent–child boundaries.

You can have OCD as a parent and successfully engage in authoritative parenting. In my experience, most parents with OCD excel at providing their children with the warmth and responsiveness that kids need to feel seen and heard. Having experienced difficult emotions yourself, you can provide your children with validation about their own experiences. However, with OCD, you may experience confusion about how best to set boundaries with your child or how to interact without symptoms taking over. You may even find yourself in a role reversal, with your child providing care for you at times. Because children are often eager to please—and fail to understand how symptom accommodation contributes to the obsessive-compulsive cycle—they can end up responding to parents in a way that exacerbates symptoms. Symptom accommodation can take the form of kids changing their behavior to assuage parental anxiety, providing reassurance, participating in rituals, supporting a parent's avoidance, sidestepping emotionally difficult topics with parents, or otherwise doing their part to "protect" the parent.

Arjun's Story

Arjun, the seventeen-year-old son of my client Priya, described how it felt easier to him to accommodate his mother's symptoms than to face the anxiety she would feel otherwise. Priya had real-event OCD, a symptom subtype that involves obsessions about an event that has occurred in the past and compulsive attempts to analyze the situation to attain certainty or prevent further consequences. When Arjun was a baby, Priya was carrying him across an icy sidewalk and slipped to the ground. Neither Arjun nor his mother was seriously injured, and both received clean bills of health at the doctor's office. However, years later when Arjun got a concussion playing soccer and lost consciousness, Priya became concerned that she must have caused her son permanent brain damage when he was a baby, which was now exacerbated by the soccer injury. She began administering a checklist of postconcussive symptoms to Arjun multiple times per week, even well after his symptoms had subsided. He went along with this process, even though his father and he recognized that it was unusual. Arjun provided his mother with reassurance that he wasn't experiencing any symptoms and even tried to persuade her that the fall as a baby didn't seem to have affected him. Priya took Arjun to three different doctors for a second opinion but was often too emotional to speak of the injury herself. Arjun was her mouthpiece and would calmly convey his mother's concerns. Finally, sad to see his mother so distressed, Arjun quit the soccer team so that she wouldn't have to worry about other injuries.

This is an extreme example of accommodation, in which a child gives up something in their own life to make their parent feel better. In this particular case, Priya and Arjun were eventually able to talk about how each was simply acting in a way that they felt would protect the other (their love for one another was unmistakable, but OCD had hijacked this affection into playing by its rules). Over time, Priya not only allowed Arjun to play soccer again but also went to his games to cheer him on.

If you find yourself in this kind of role reversal, don't beat yourself up. Know that your awareness of this pattern is the first step to changing things. Let your child know that they don't need to be your caretaker and that you are going to help them step out of that role. This conversation can vary based on your child's developmental stage and your comfort with talking to them about your OCD. With older children, sharing information about your diagnosis may help to give them additional context about your behavior. Younger children may benefit from something simpler, such as hearing that you're working on your worries.

OCD in Children

OCD has a genetic component, though it's certainly not as simple as having a single gene that causes the condition. Instead, there are multiple factors that influence the development and expression of OCD throughout the life span. We do know that if you have OCD, your kids are more likely to have OCD than if you didn't have OCD. We also know that if you first showed signs of OCD before puberty, you're more likely than someone with adult-onset OCD to have biological children with obsessive-compulsive symptoms. But in either case, the likelihood is nowhere near 100 percent; in fact, the odds are considerably higher that your child won't have OCD symptoms (Pauls et al. 2014). The kicker is that there's no one perfect formula to predict whether your child will have OCD based on your diagnosis alone.

Of course, uncertainty is a hotbed for OCD, and in the guilty-until-proven-innocent spirit that OCD often invokes, many parents who choose to have biological children worry that they'll "cause" their child's OCD through either their biology or their parenting style. This concern is often tinged with shame, doubt, and the familiar twist of inflated responsibility. So, it's important to say up front: if you have a child with OCD (or if you'll someday have a child with OCD), you are not the cause of your child's OCD, and beating yourself up is not the solution. In fact, you of all people are uniquely poised to help your child navigate their disorder from a perspective of empathy, compassion, and skillfulness.

There are a number of books written for parents of children with OCD, so this section will provide only a brief overview of some skills you can use with your child. Unsurprisingly, there's a large body of research about the role of accommodation in families of children with OCD. Parental participation in rituals, elimination of children's responsibilities, or other attempts to promote avoidance may feel good in the moment but have long-term negative effects on your child's well-being. As you know, when you receive accommodation from others, it temporarily scratches the compulsive itch but shrinks your world over time. The same goes for kids. Research from the Supportive Parenting for Anxious Childhood Emotions (SPACE) program, a parent-based intervention developed at Yale, indicates that reductions in parental accommodation of child symptoms alone can reduce OCD symptoms, even if the child never works with a therapist one-on-one (Lebowitz et al. 2020). Therefore, nipping accommodation in the bud is an important part of supporting your child's recovery from OCD.

While it's hard not to provide reassurance for a distraught little one, you can choose to empower them by validating their big emotions and expressing your confidence in their ability to tolerate them. This may look like kneeling down beside your crying child who's begging you to tell them that they won't get sick and saying, "Wow, that's a big emotion you're having there. I know how hard it is, and I know that you can get through it. If I tell you that you won't get sick, I'll be making the worry monster even bigger, so let's not give the monster what it wants now."

This kind of a script can be altered based on the child's developmental level; it conveys to them that you understand their distress and that you'll provide support so long as it's not accommodation. Metaphors like the worry monster or the OCD plant being watered by compulsions work well for younger kids. It may be more appropriate with teens to afford them the opportunity to discuss their symptoms and to come up with their own metaphors. You may want to ask questions about what life would look like without OCD to highlight for them what they're missing by engaging in compulsions and avoidance. And, given that you'll always be a parent first and not a mental health counselor, it's helpful to have a therapist on board to provide support and accountability.

Although disclosure is certainly a personal decision for each family, I strongly encourage you to tell your children if you too have OCD. Such disclosure helps kids feel validated and fight the stigma of mental health concerns as shameful or embarrassing. Disclosure also creates a general family culture of honesty and openness, which promotes trust. Given that many kids instinctively try to hide their symptoms, talking openly about your own can encourage them to open up as well.

You can model to them what has worked for you or just model your own bravery in the face of uncertainty and anxiety. Every time you challenge a thought aloud or label an emotion that you're experiencing, kids are learning skills they too can use. Teach them that they can experience fear and cope with it, and that this is the true meaning of bravery. The parent of a six-year-old with OCD recently told me about how her son's hard work on fighting just right and contamination symptoms helped her to take some risks. It's okay to inspire and be inspired by one another!

Way to Go, Parents!

If you have kids, I want to praise you for your dedication to the difficult and important job of raising little ones. Kudos to you for taking the time to read this chapter and improve your relationships with your children! Next, we'll shift from the hard work of parenting to the hard work of, well, work itself. Managing your relationships with others at work depends on many factors, such as the nature of your industry, opportunities for collaboration, and the social climate of your workplace. We'll discuss how best to cultivate positive relationships and how to use these connections to promote support and advocacy.

CHAPTER 10

Nine-to-Five
Relationships at Work

There are many different levels of intimacy in relationships, and we've covered most in this book, from romantic partners to roommates to children. This chapter moves on to an area of your life where you may spend significant time but don't always have significant relationships: work. Considering the traditional eight-hour workday and two-day weekend structure, our time at work really adds up. In fact, while you're employed full time, you're likely to spend almost a quarter of your hours on the clock. So, it's a bonus if you have harmonious relationships with your colleagues. And although your contact with others may vary, the relationships you develop at work can help you feel successful and enhance your sense of belonging. Not to mention, with OCD burrowing itself into anything important, symptoms frequently pop up on the job. Having strong relationships can provide emotional support, increase motivation to reduce symptoms, and help you to advocate for yourself authentically.

While some relationships at work are like friendships—based on choice and mutual interest—others are determined by the employment structure itself. I'll be concentrating on the latter kind here since they're not covered elsewhere in the book. We'll review different types of work relationships, what your rights are as an employee, and how to put your skills into action in this environment.

When You Have OCD at Work

Recall that OCD loves to attack things that are valuable to you. So, as you probably appreciate being able to pay your bills, work is a natural environment for OCD to infiltrate and thrive. This can be exacerbated if your profession feels meaningful or is a large part of your identity. On the job, there's room for any theme to pop up: perfectionism and just right symptoms in work tasks, ROCD in relationships with supervisors, or contamination worries about that nasty shelf in the cleaned-twice-yearly refrigerator…yikes! And even if OCD is generally quiet at work, having a difficult day can throw things off quickly. Getting a little behind snowballs into getting a lot behind, and then your self-critical tendencies join the party too. You might think: *Everyone else is just chugging along, and I'm the only one struggling.* You want to reach out, but your colleagues don't know about your OCD, and you don't want to be judged by people who might not understand what it's like to wrestle with your own thoughts. So you put your nose to the proverbial grindstone and keep going, but it sure would be nicer not to have to do it in isolation.

My heart rate went up just writing that paragraph! The impact of OCD on work, an environment in which there are natural opportunities for evaluation and scrutiny, can be significant and significantly distressing. If you've been in this situation, I want you to know how incredibly common it is for people with OCD to struggle at work. I've served clients in diverse professions and have witnessed firsthand their complex feelings about how to address work-related OCD symptoms while maintaining appropriate and supportive relationships there. A study of women with OCD in the workplace found that many participants reported difficulties, including trouble finding work and issues with misunderstandings of their symptoms by their superiors (Neal-Barnett and Mendelson 2003). If OCD is left untreated or if it's poorly understood by those in positions of power, the fallout from OCD can stunt growth in your career and can even lead to job termination. Thankfully, there are legal protections for employees with OCD that require employers to provide reasonable accommodations to help you thrive at work. We'll discuss these legal protections later in the chapter, but first let's explore the different kinds of relationships you might have at work and how to make them work for you.

Relationships on the Job

Work relationships come in three relationship tiers: seniors, peers, and juniors. Seniors are your bosses, supervisors, or managers; they oversee you or monitor your performance. As evaluators of your work and signers of paychecks, seniors have some authority over you. They may also be mentors, imparting professional wisdom or skills along the way. Peers are the other people in your organization who have similar roles and neither supervise nor receive supervision from you. You may share a common boss or work in parallel positions in separate departments. Peers resemble you in experience and responsibilities and may collaborate with you on projects. Juniors are those who directly report to you or whose performance you evaluate in some way. You are responsible for making sure that they're meeting expectations, and you may also strive to keep work a safe, happy, and fulfilling place for them. Each kind of relationship has its own structure and social customs, and managing each takes different skills.

YOUR RELATIONSHIPS WITH SENIORS

Maintaining a good relationship with your boss can feel tricky when you have OCD. In some ways, the relationship is transactional, with roles defined by the employment agreement itself. On the other hand, depending on your field and workplace culture, there may be emotional intimacy as well (just try working with a bunch of therapists!). Figuring out how to manage your relationship with a supervisor can start with clarifying whether and how OCD impacts you at work. It could be something directly related to performance, like taking longer to complete documentation due to checking, or it could be more relational, like not attending the annual work picnic because of contamination fears.

In some cases, disclosure may be helpful. Again, your decision to disclose depends partly on whether a disclosure can provide context for your behavior and if that context would be helpful. You don't owe your seniors an explanation for why you're not attending an optional social event. However, it may be more beneficial to provide some context for difficulties completing tasks or inconsistencies of work. With disclosure, your behavior is less likely to be interpreted as an indicator of low motivation, commitment, or interest. Moreover, you can then collaborate with your supervisor on a plan so that you can meet your potential and contribute.

If your boss is also a mentor, you may want to talk about your OCD not because it measurably affects your work but because it's a large part of who you are. Consider their past reactions to any vulnerable information you've shared or if they've demonstrated sensitivity to mental health concerns more broadly. If they've been open and kind in these types of interactions, they're more likely to respond similarly here.

RELATIONSHIPS WITH PEERS

Our coworkers can substantially affect our workplace satisfaction. Working with people who provide practical and emotional support lightens the mood and helps to alleviate stress on the job. Conversely, working with people who are disrespectful of your time, space, beliefs, or behavior can make for an inhospitable environment. If you're a people pleaser, it can be tough to recognize the latter situation and stand up for yourself. Your OCD may also try to convince you that it's only because of your symptoms that you're bothered by others' behaviors. Because you don't choose your coworkers any more than you choose your own family, many of the strategies from chapter 8 will be useful here. If OCD affects your ability to collaborate with peers, you may consider disclosure to clear up any misunderstandings or assumptions. You can also design values-based exposures to help you increase positive work behaviors while whittling down your compulsions. You can use the "Workplace Exposure Hierarchy" available at http://www.newharbinger.com/50584. Remember to think about which values are most important for you to demonstrate at work before coming up with your exposures. Then get to whittling away at your anxiety and getting back to your values!

RELATIONSHIPS WITH JUNIORS

People with OCD can make for kind, attentive, and supportive bosses. Many clients have beamed with pride in our sessions when talking about mentoring juniors on the job. But having authority over others can provoke symptoms as well. With moral scrupulosity, you may compulsively scrutinize your own behavior to ensure that it is unfailingly ethical. With just right concerns, you may struggle with accepting employees who deviate from your preferred protocols. As a reassurance seeker, you may doubt the positive feedback that you receive from others and look for ways to calm your own performance concerns. This can come out as repetitive questions about whether your juniors feel respected or whether they think you're supportive enough. As with any other relationship, what you do to lessen the impact of OCD depends on your particular worries. If you're worried about perfectionism in mentoring, remember that being human is also a wonderful thing to model for juniors. Practice flexibility as you help your juniors find their own way to complete tasks. Learn to delegate tasks that you're worried won't be done just right and resist the urge to seek reassurance from your employees outside of intervals determined by your job structure.

Aiden's Story

Aiden, a twenty-nine-year-old nonbinary insurance agent with existential OCD, fixated on unknowable questions about the nature of reality and free will. Aiden had read multiple philosophical texts and articles about these topics, seeking information about simulation

theories, and searching for evidence to determine "irrefutably" that we
have free will. At times, Aiden's compulsions interfered with work;
researching would lead to arriving late to the office, and ruminating
during the day would lead to staying late. Aiden told me that they
tried to keep a low profile at work, as having their boss and coworkers
use their pronouns already felt like an imposition for the somewhat
conservative company where they worked. Telling others about their
mental health concerns just seemed like one more way to stand out.

However, Aiden found that they had no choice after their boss,
Petra, witnessed them having a panic attack during a one-on-one
meeting. Aiden had been browsing social media over lunch and found
an article about neurological changes that occur in the brain
milliseconds before we make decisions. Aiden took the findings in this
article to mean that people have only the illusion of making choices
and therefore don't have free will. They began frantically trying to
think of other explanations to assuage their anxiety before they were
interrupted by a knock on the door. Petra poked her head in, and
Aiden realized that they had lost track of time. "I thought we were
meeting in my office, but we can meet here," Petra said, sitting down
opposite Aiden.

When Petra made the offhand comment, "I don't feel like we
have any choice" about a recent policy change, Aiden's OCD kicked
into overdrive. They began breathing rapidly and tearing up,
eventually leaving the room to go to the bathroom. When they came
back bleary-eyed and embarrassed, Aiden assured Petra that this was
an unusual occurrence and apologized for "being unprofessional."
Petra was kind and understanding in response, disclosing that she too
had experienced a few panic attacks and knew how uncomfortable
they were. While Aiden didn't want to disclose the nature of their
symptoms, they mentioned having anxiety and sometimes taking
breaks during the day to manage it. "That's why I'm sometimes
working late even though I know I'm supposed to clock out by five
o'clock," they told her. Petra was shocked to hear this and had

assumed that Aiden's troubles with maintaining a consistent schedule reflected a lackluster commitment to the job. She had difficulty reconciling this with Aiden's job performance and sales data, however, which were consistently impressive. Aiden's disclosure helped to explain how Aiden could be such a good employee but also seem so aloof at times.

Petra was able to create a more flexible time structure for Aiden, absolving them of the usual clocking-in-and-out obligations. This event brought them closer, and Aiden felt less stressed at work.

Not everyone is fortunate enough to have a boss like Petra. Let's explore what you can do to advocate for yourself if your working environment is less flexible.

Exercising Your Rights

There are many potential advantages to disclosing your OCD at work, including improved relationships, authenticity, and environmental support (Brouwers et al. 2020). But if you feel reluctant to share anything about OCD at work, you're in good company. Commonly cited reasons include worries about stigma and social rejection at work, both of which, unfortunately, sometimes happen. However, you likely have legal rights to nondiscrimination in your workplace. If you work in the United States and your company is large enough (fifteen or more employees), you have protections as an employee under the Americans with Disabilities Act (ADA). Under the ADA, people with permanent or long-lasting limitations whose symptoms considerably affect them but who are still able to fulfill the primary functions of their job are eligible to receive accommodations. Many other countries have protective laws in place with similar provisions. For example, Canada and Australia both have laws preventing employers from taking adverse actions against employees with mental health diagnoses.

This book has emphasized how certain accommodations can be harmful in the long run for OCD (see the entirety of chapter 2), but sometimes accommodations can help you to better complete your job duties. ADA accommodations, like providing someone who uses a wheelchair with access to a ramp and an accessible workstation, exist not to give anyone an advantage over others but to ensure that there are equitable conditions for all workers. Similarly, accommodations for OCD can allow you to complete your job without being penalized for also having symptoms. You may also qualify for paid medical leave from work to engage in intensive or residential treatment. In the United States, this falls under the Family and Medical Leave Act (FMLA) and is eligible to anyone who has worked for at least a year at a company with fifty or more employees. While the paperwork can be lengthy and time away from work can be scary, it's worth it to be able to put your mental health first.

Go Forth and Connect!

As challenging as it can be to live with OCD—tormented by endless thought loops and pulled into frustrating rituals—it's even more challenging to do so without the support of others. I hope that after reading this book, you feel more empowered to seek out relationships, strengthen the ones you already have, and advocate for yourself with others. It has been an honor to share this time with you, and I'm thankful for the relationship we've built through these pages.

References

Abramowitz, J. S., D. H. Baucom, M. G. Wheaton, S. Boeding, L. E. Fabricant, C. Paprocki, and M. S. Fischer. 2013. "Enhancing Exposure and Response Prevention for OCD: A Couple-Based Approach." *Behavior Modification* 37 (2): 189–210.

Albert, U., A. Baffa, and G. Maina. 2017. "Family Accommodation in Adult Obsessive-Compulsive Disorder: Clinical Perspectives." *Psychology Research and Behavior Management* 10: 293–304.

Basson, R., S. Leiblum, L. Brotto, L. Derogatis, J. Fourcroy, K. Fugl-Meyer, A. Graziottin, J. R. Heiman, E. Laan, C. Meston, L. Schover, J. Van Lankveld, and W. Weijmar Shultz. 2004. "Revised Definitions of Women's Sexual Dysfunction." *The Journal of Sexual Medicine* 1 (1): 40–48.

Bertera, E. M. 2005. "Mental Health in US Adults: The Role of Positive Social Support and Social Negativity in Personal Relationships." *Journal of Social and Personal Relationships* 22 (1): 33–48.

Borda, T., B. A. Feinstein, F. Neziroglu, T. Veccia, and R. Pérez-Rivera. 2013. "Are Children with Obsessive-Compulsive Disorder at Risk for Problematic Peer Relationships?" *Journal of Obsessive-Compulsive and Related Disorders* 2 (4): 359–65.

Bouvard, M., N. Fournet, A. Denis, A. Sixdenier, and D. Clark. 2017. "Intrusive Thoughts in Patients with Obsessive Compulsive Disorder and Non-Clinical Participants: A Comparison Using the International Intrusive Thought Interview Schedule." *Cognitive Behaviour Therapy* 46 (4): 287–99.

Brotto, L. A. 2018. *Better Sex Through Mindfulness: How Women Can Cultivate Desire.* Vancouver, British Columbia: Greystone Books.

Brouwers, E. P. M., M.C. W. Joosen, C. van Zelst, C., and J. Van Weeghel. 2020. "To Disclose or Not to Disclose: A Multi-Stakeholder Focus Group Study on Mental Health Issues in the Work Environment." *Journal of Occupational Rehabilitation* 30 (1): 84–92.

Buchholz, J. L., S. N. Hellberg, and J. S. Abramowitz 2020. "Phenomenology of Perinatal Obsessive-Compulsive Disorder." In *Biomarkers of Postpartum Psychiatric Disorders,* edited by J. L. Payne and L. M. Osborne, 79–83. Cambridge, MA: Academic Press.

Doron, G., D. S. Derby, O. Szepsenwol, and D. Talmor. 2012. "Tainted Love: Exploring Relationship-Centered Obsessive Compulsive Symptoms in Two Non-Clinical Cohorts." *Journal of Obsessive-Compulsive and Related Disorders* 1 (1): 16–24.

Feldman, R., C.W. Greenbaum, and N. Yirmiya. 1999. "Mother–Infant Affect Synchrony as an Antecedent of the Emergence of Self-Control." *Developmental Psychology* 35 (1): 223–31.

Geller, D. A., S. Homayoun, and G. Johnson. 2021. "Developmental Considerations in Obsessive Compulsive Disorder: Comparing Pediatric and Adult-Onset Cases." *Frontiers in Psychiatry* 12: 678538.

Gottman, J., and J. Gottman. 2017. "The Natural Principles of Love." *Journal of Family Theory and Review* 9 (1): 7–26.

Gwilliam, P., A. Wells, and S. Cartwright-Hatton. 2004. "Does Meta-Cognition or Responsibility Predict Obsessive-Compulsive Symptoms: A Test of the Metacognitive Model." *Clinical Psychology and Psychotherapy* 11 (2): 137–44.

Halldorsson, B., P. M. Salkovskis, O. Kobori, and R. Pagdin. 2016. "I Do Not Know What Else to Do: Caregivers' Perspective on Reassurance Seeking in OCD." *Journal of Obsessive-Compulsive and Related Disorders* 8: 21–30.

Hershfield, J. 2015. *When a Family Member Has OCD: Mindfulness and Cognitive Behavioral Skills to Help Families Affected by Obsessive-Compulsive Disorder.* Oakland, CA: New Harbinger Publications.

Himle, J. A., R. J. Taylor, A. W. Nguyen, M. T. Williams, K. D. Lincoln, H. O. Taylor, and L. M. Chatters. 2017. "Family and Friendship Networks and Obsessive-Compulsive Disorder Among African Americans and Black Caribbeans." *The Behavior Therapist* 40 (3): 99–105.

Kagan, E. R., H. E. Frank, and P. C. Kendall. 2017. "Accommodation in Youth with OCD and Anxiety." *Clinical Psychology: Science and Practice* 24 (1): 78–98.

Kent de Grey, R. G., and B. N. Uchino. 2020. "The Health Correlates and Consequences of Friendship." In *The Wiley Encyclopedia of Health Psychology*, vol. 2, edited by K. Sweeny, M. L. Robbins, and L. M. Cohen. Hoboken, NJ: John Wiley and Sons.

Koolwal, A., S. Agarwal, S. Manohar, G. D. Koolwal, and A. Gupta. 2020. "Obsessive-Compulsive Disorder and Sexuality: A Narrative Review." *Journal of Psychosexual Health* 2 (1): 37–43.

Lebowitz, E. R., C. Marin, A. Martino, Y. Shimshoni, and W. K. Silverman. 2020. "Parent-Based Treatment as Efficacious as Cognitive-Behavioral Therapy for Childhood Anxiety: A Randomized Noninferiority Study of Supportive Parenting for Anxious Childhood Emotions." *Journal of the American Academy of Child and Adolescent Psychiatry* 59 (3): 362–72.

Lebowitz, E. R., K. E. Panza, and M. H. Bloch. 2016. "Family Accommodation in Obsessive-Compulsive and Anxiety Disorders: A Five-Year Update." *Expert Review of Neurotherapeutics* 16 (1): 45–53.

Lee, E., D. Steinberg, L. Phillips, J. Hart, A. Smith, and C. Wetterneck. 2015. "Examining the Effects of Accommodation and Caregiver Burden on Relationship Satisfaction in Caregivers of Individuals with OCD." *Bulletin of the Menninger Clinic* 79 (1): 1–13.

MacDowall, W., K. G. Jones, C. Tanton, S. Clifton, A. J. Copas, C. H. Mercer, M. J. Palmer, R. Lewis, J. Datta, K. R. Mitchell, N. Field, P. Sonnenberg, A. M. Johnson, and K. Wellings. 2015. "Associations Between Source of Information About Sex and Sexual Health Outcomes in Britain: Findings from the Third National Survey of Sexual Attitudes and Lifestyles (Natsal-3)." *BMJ Open* 5 (3): e007837.

Masters, W., and V. E. Johnson. 1970. *Human Sexual Inadequacy.* New York: Little, Brown and Company

McConnell, A. R., E. Paige Lloyd, and B. T. Humphrey. 2019. "We Are Family: Viewing Pets as Family Members Improves Wellbeing." *Anthrozoös* 32 (4): 459–70.

McLeod, B. D., J. J. Wood, and J. R. Weisz. 2007. "Examining the Association Between Parenting and Childhood Anxiety: A Meta-Analysis." *Clinical Psychology Review* 27 (2): 155–72.

Melli, G., F. Bulli, G. Doron, and C. Carraresi. 2018. "Maladaptive Beliefs in Relationship Obsessive Compulsive Disorder (ROCD): Replication and Extension in a Clinical Sample." *Journal of Obsessive-Compulsive and Related Disorders* 18: 47–53.

Miller, W. R., and G. S. Rose. 2015. "Motivational Interviewing and Decisional Balance: Contrasting Responses to Client Ambivalence." *Behavioural and Cognitive Psychotherapy* 43 (2): 129–41.

Nagoski, E. 2015. *Come as You Are: The Surprising New Science That Will Transform Your Sex Life.* New York: Simon and Schuster.

Neal-Barnett, A., and L. L. Mendelson. 2003. "Obsessive Compulsive Disorder in the Workplace: An Invisible Disability." *Women and Therapy* 26 (1): 169–78.

Neff, K. 2021. *Fierce Self-Compassion: How Women Can Harness Kindness to Speak Up, Claim Their Power, and Thrive.* New York: HarperCollins.

Norman, L. J., S. F. Taylor, Y. Liu, J. Radua, Y. Chye, Y., S. J. De Wit, C. Huyser, F. I. Karahanoglu, T. Luks, D. Manoach, C. Mathews, K. Rubia, C. Suo, O. A. van den Heuvel, M. Yücel, and K. Fitzgerald. 2019. "Error Processing and Inhibitory Control in Obsessive-Compulsive Disorder: A Meta-Analysis Using Statistical Parametric Maps." *Biological Psychiatry* 85 (9): 713–25.

Olatunji, B. O., H. Berg, R. C. Cox, and A. Billingsley. 2017. "The Effects of Cognitive Reappraisal on Conditioned Disgust in Contamination-Based OCD: An Analogue Study." *Journal of Anxiety Disorders* 51: 86–93.

Olatunji, B. O., M. L. Davis, M. B. Powers, and J. A. Smits. 2013. "Cognitive-Behavioral Therapy for Obsessive-Compulsive Disorder: A Meta-Analysis of Treatment Outcome and Moderators." *Journal of Psychiatric Research* 47 (1): 33–41.

Pauls, D. L., A. Abramovitch, S. L. Rauch, and D. A. Geller. 2014. "Obsessive–Compulsive Disorder: An Integrative Genetic and Neurobiological Perspective." *Nature Reviews Neuroscience* 15 (6): 410–24.

Peris, T. S., C. A. Sugar, R. L. Bergman, S. Chang, A. Langley, and J. Piacentini. 2012. "Family Factors Predict Treatment Outcome for Pediatric Obsessive-Compulsive Disorder." *Journal of Consulting and Clinical Psychology* 80 (2): 255–63.

Pinciotti, C. M., Z. Smith, S. Singh, C. T. Wetterneck, and M. T. Williams. 2022. "Call to Action: Recommendations for Justice-Based Treatment of Obsessive-Compulsive Disorder with Sexual Orientation and Gender Themes." *Behavior Therapy* 53 (2): 153–69.

Pinquart, M., and R. Kauser. 2018. "Do the Associations of Parenting Styles with Behavior Problems and Academic Achievement Vary by Culture? Results from a Meta-Analysis." *Cultural Diversity and Ethnic Minority Psychology* 24 (1): 75–100.

Ruscio, A., D. Stein, W. Chiu, and R. C. Kessler. 2010. "The Epidemiology of Obsessive-Compulsive Disorder in the National Comorbidity Survey Replication." *Molecular Psychiatry* 15 (1): 53–63.

Simpson, J. A., S. W. Rholes, and D. Phillips. 1996. "Conflict in Close Relationships: An Attachment Perspective." *Journal of Personality and Social Psychology* 71 (5): 899–914.

Solem, S., A. T. Haaland, K. Hagen, G. Launes, B. Hansen, P. A. Vogel, and J. A. Himle. 2015. "Interpersonal Style in Obsessive Compulsive Disorder." *The Cognitive Behaviour Therapist* 8 (29): 1–17.

Stewart, K. E., D. Sumantry, and B. L. Malivoire. 2020. "Family and Couple Integrated Cognitive-Behavioural Therapy for Adults with OCD: A Meta-Analysis." *Journal of Affective Disorders* 277: 159–68.

Stoddard, J. A., and N. Afari. 2014. *The Big Book of ACT Metaphors: A Practitioner's Guide to Experiential Exercises and Metaphors in Acceptance and Commitment Therapy.* Oakland, CA: New Harbinger Publications.

Twohig, M. P., J. S. Abramowitz, B. M. Smith, L. E. Fabricant, R. J. Jacoby, K. L. Morrison, E. J. Bluett, L. Reuman, S. M. Blakey, and T. Ledermann. 2018. "Adding Acceptance and Commitment Therapy to Exposure and Response Prevention for Obsessive-Compulsive Disorder: A Randomized Controlled Trial." *Behaviour Research and Therapy* 108: 1–9.

Van Leeuwen, W. A., G. A. Van Wingen, P. Luyten, D. Denys, and H. J. F. Van Marle. 2020. "Attachment in OCD: A Meta-Analysis." *Journal of Anxiety Disorders* 70: 102187.

Wenzlaff, R. M., and D. M. Wegner. 2000. "Thought Suppression." *Annual Review of Psychology* 51: 59–91.

Werner-Seidler, A., M. H. Afzali, C. Chapman, M. Sunderland, and T. Slade. 2017. "The Relationship Between Social Support Networks and Depression in the 2007 National Survey of Mental Health and Well-Being." *Social Psychiatry and Psychiatric Epidemiology* 52 (12): 1463–73.

Williams, M., M. Debreaux, and M. Jahn. 2016. "African Americans with Obsessive-Compulsive Disorder: An Update." *Current Psychiatry Reviews* 12: 109–14.

Williams, M. T., C. Wetterneck, G. Tellawi, and G. Duque. 2015. "Domains of Distress Among People with Sexual Orientation Obsessions." *Archives of Sexual Behavior* 44 (3): 783–89.

Wu, M. S., J. F. McGuire, C. Martino, V. Phares, R. R. Selles, and E. A. Storch. 2016. "A Meta-Analysis of Family Accommodation and OCD Symptom Severity." *Clinical Psychology Review* 45: 34–44.

Ziegler, S., K. Bednasch, S. Baldofski, and C. Rummel-Kluge. 2021. "Long Durations from Symptom Onset to Diagnosis and from Diagnosis to Treatment in Obsessive-Compulsive Disorder: A Retrospective Self-Report Study." *PLoS One* 16 (12): e0261169.

Amy Mariaskin, PhD, is a licensed clinical psychologist with fifteen years of experience treating obsessive-compulsive disorder (OCD), anxiety, and related disorders. She is founding director of the Nashville OCD & Anxiety Treatment Center, faculty of the International OCD Foundation's Behavior Therapy Training Institute, and adjunct professor at Vanderbilt University. Mariaskin has provided individual and group therapy to adults, adolescents, children, and families affected by these disorders. She strives to create a sensitive and affirming therapeutic experience for her clients, and incorporates humor and creativity into evidence-based practice.

Foreword writer **Kimberley Quinlan, LMFT,** is a psychotherapist in private practice specializing in the treatment of obsessive-compulsive disorder (OCD) and related disorders. She is host of the *Your Anxiety Toolkit* podcast, and founder of www.cbtschool.com—an online psychoeducation platform for OCD, anxiety disorders, and body-focused repetitive behaviors (BFRBs).

Real change *is* possible

For more than forty-five years, New Harbinger has published proven-effective self-help books and pioneering workbooks to help readers of all ages and backgrounds improve mental health and well-being, and achieve lasting personal growth. In addition, our spirituality books offer profound guidance for deepening awareness and cultivating healing, self-discovery, and fulfillment.

Founded by psychologist Matthew McKay and Patrick Fanning, New Harbinger is proud to be an independent, employee-owned company. Our books reflect our core values of integrity, innovation, commitment, sustainability, compassion, and trust. Written by leaders in the field and recommended by therapists worldwide, New Harbinger books are practical, accessible, and provide real tools for real change.

newharbingerpublications

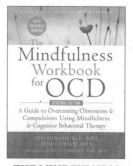
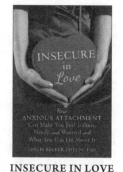

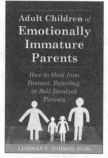

Did you know there are **free tools** you can download for this book?

Free tools are things like **worksheets, guided meditation exercises**, and **more** that will help you get the most out of your book.

You can download free tools for this book— whether you bought or borrowed it, in any format, from any source—from the New Harbinger website. All you need is a NewHarbinger.com account. Just use the URL provided in this book to view the free tools that are available for it. Then, click on the "download" button for the free tool you want, and follow the prompts that appear to log in to your NewHarbinger.com account and download the material.

You can also save the free tools for this book to your **Free Tools Library** so you can access them again anytime, just by logging in to your account! Just look for this button on the book's free tools page.

+ Save this to my free tools library

If you need help accessing or downloading free tools, visit **newharbinger.com/faq** or contact us at **customerservice@newharbinger.com**.